CAREER

DISCOVERY

ENCYCLOPEDIA

VOLUME 6
Scu — Zoo

FERGUSON PUBLISHING COMPANY
Chicago

3 4162 00022 1349

Career discovery encyclopedia / [Carol J. Summerfield, editor-in-chief].
        p.   cm.
    Includes indexes.
    Summary: Six volumes with 504 articles on all categories of occupations with such information as description of the job, earnings, educational and training requirements, addresses to get more information, and other pertinent facts.
    ISBN 0-89434-144-8 (set) : $119.95
    1. Vocational guidance—Dictionaries—Juvenile literature. [1. Vocational guidance—Dictionaries   2. Occupations.]
I. Summerfield, Carol J., 1960–
HF5381.2.C37   1993
331.7′02′03—dc20   92–32314
                                                              CIP
                                                              AC

Manufactured in the United States of America
R-1

Contents

Key to Symbols

 Professional, Administrative, and Managerial Occupations Jobs that require much preparation and training and involve a high level of mental activity. These people must apply theory to solve practical problems. They often direct people who are working together to achieve specific goals.

 Clerical Occupations Jobs that involve keeping records and accounts, filing papers, handling correspondence and other kinds of communications, and performing other routine work in offices such as those in business, government, and education.

 Sales Occupations Jobs that involve selling goods, services, or property on a retail or wholesale basis, including jobs as agents or brokers. In addition to selling, people in sales occupations often provide sales-related services to customers and may plan what products to sell and how to sell them.

 Service Occupations Jobs that involve assisting people with personal needs or daily activities. Workers typically prepare and serve food in restaurants, maintain buildings, provide grooming and health care services, and such. Also, jobs that protect lives and property, such as those in law enforcement.

 Agricultural, Forestry, and Conservation Occupations Jobs that involve outdoor work and the use and maintenance of the natural environment. Activities related to farming, ranching, fishing, hunting animals, caring for parks and gardens, logging, and some mining operations are included.

 Processing Occupations Jobs that involve purifying, blending, treating, or working with a wide range of materials, from foods to industrial products like paper or paint. To prepare these materials, workers use such equipment as vats, ovens, furnaces, mixers, grinders, filters, and molders.

 Machines Trades Occupations Jobs that involve operating machines to cut, shape, and work materials such as metals, plastics, wood, paper, and stone. Some jobs require being familiar with the details of how the machines work, reading blueprints, and making computations for adjusting machine functions.

 **Bench Work Occupations** Jobs that involve using hand tools and machines mounted on a bench or table in a workshop. Workers make or repair small products such as jewelry, clothes, shoes, instruments, or lenses. They cut pieces to size, fit parts together, and inspect finished items.

 Structural Work Occupations Jobs, usually outdoors, in constructing or repairing bridges, roads, buildings; installing telephone or communications equipment; or assembling structures. Also, jobs on factory production lines constructing motor vehicles, boilers, or large machines and equipment.

 **Language Arts** Jobs that emphasize verbal and written communications, such as English, translating, and journalism.

 Social Sciences Jobs that emphasize interactive and interpersonal skills, such as social work, political science, anthropology, and wildlife management.

 **Manual Skills** Jobs that emphasize dexterity, coordination, such as bench and construction trades.

 **Sciences and Mathematics** Jobs that emphasize linear and abstract reasoning, such as physics, chemistry, biology, and medicine.

 **Arts** Jobs that emphasize creative interpretation, such as music, art, design, and dance.

 People Skills Jobs that emphasize leadership, management, congeniality, and teamwork, such as bank tellers, post office employees, and restaurant servers.

 **Organizational Skills** Jobs that emphasize resource structuring skills, such as accounting and clerical work.

Sculptors and Ceramists

Other articles to look at:
▶ **Artists and Painters**
▶ **Ceramic Engineers**
▶ **Commercial Artists**

What sculptors and ceramists do

Sculptors and *ceramists* are people who work with ceramic materials to create products of great usefulness or beauty. Because of their abundance and durability, ceramic materials are used in an amazing variety of products, including pottery, sculpture, dinnerware, building materials, and cement. Though individuals interested in ceramics may consider careers in industry and research, as well as in the fine arts, this article deals primarily with ceramic artists.

Ceramic artists may choose to create either pottery, which is intended to be functional as well as attractive, or sculpture, which is primarily decorative. Though the two categories overlap considerably, artists who make pots intended for use are usually called potters; those who create nonfunctional, or decorative pieces, are referred to as sculptors.

Before shaping the clay, both potters and sculptors must prepare the clay through a process called wedging. Wedging is accomplished by kneading the clay, or by repeatedly throwing it down on a flat surface. This process distributes moisture evenly throughout the clay, and forces any hidden air bubbles to the surface.

Artists generally shape the clay in one of two ways: by hand building, or by using a potter's wheel. Hand building allows the artist greater freedom in forming the clay, and is often preferred for sculptural works. The spinning motion of the potter's wheel enables the artist to create the symmetrical forms traditionally favored for functional vessels, such as vases or bowls.

In hand building, the artist may flatten the clay, to form slabs, or roll it out into coils. To attach the separate pieces of clay, the artist uses a sharp tool to scratch, or score, the surfaces to be joined, then cements them together with extremely wet, muddy clay, called slip. By joining the slabs or coils, and gently shaping them into the desired form, the artist slowly builds the pot or sculpture.

When using a potter's wheel, the potter places a wedged ball of clay in the middle of the wheel. With the wheel rotating at a brisk pace, the potter pushes steadily against the clay with both hands. This process is called centering the clay. Once the clay is positioned, the potter creates an opening by pushing two fingers down into the center of the spinning clay. Then, placing the fingers of one hand inside this opening, and the fingers of the other on the outside, the potter slowly compresses the clay to begin forming the walls of the pot. In a series of pulling motions, the potter begins to move the clay upward, stretching and shaping the walls. When this process, which is called throwing the pot, is complete, the potter uses a metal wire to cut the pot from the wheel. The finished pot is set aside to dry.

Both pottery and ceramic sculpture must be baked, or fired, in a large oven called a kiln. Most ceramic work is fired twice. The first firing, which lasts approximately six hours, hardens the clay. Before the second firing, the artist will often apply a glaze to the ceramic piece. Glazes are liquid mixtures of minerals and silicates (glass-forming substances). When fired at high temperatures, glazes form a colorful, glassy surface on the ceramic piece. This second firing can last from 12 to 14 hours, and can reach temperatures of about 2,450 degrees fahrenheit, or 1,340 degrees celsius.

Education and training

While ceramic artists are not required to obtain a formal education, most find it very helpful. Individuals who wish to teach ceramics at the high school level must have a bachelor's degree in fine arts or in ceramics. A Master of Fine Arts degree is required for those who wish to teach ceramics at the college level.

Earnings

Ceramic artists rarely become wealthy. The process is extremely time-consuming, and the equipment involved can be very expensive. Some very dedicated individuals can sell enough of their work to support themselves, but most ceramic artists find that a supplemental income is necessary.

Ways of getting more information

For additional information, write to:

▶ American Ceramic Society
735 Ceramic Place
Westerville, OH 43081

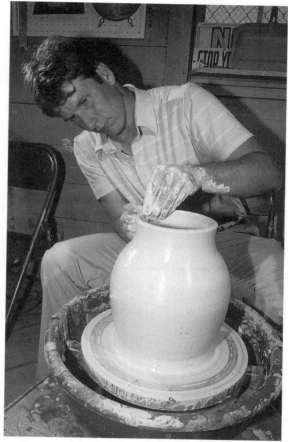

▶ A rotating wheel allows a potter to shape and stretch the clay into a pot.

▶ United States Advanced Ceramics Association
1440 New York Ave., NW., Ste. 300
Washington, DC 20005

▶ United States Potters Association
518 Market Street
East Liverpool, OH 43920

Secondary School Teachers

Other articles to look at:
- ▶ **Elementary School Teachers**
- ▶ **Guidance Counselors**
- ▶ **Librarians**
- ▶ **School Administrators**
- ▶ **Teacher Aides**

What secondary school teachers do

Secondary school teachers instruct junior and senior high school students. They often specialize in a certain subject, such as English, mathematics, biology, or history but may also teach several subjects. In addition to classroom instruction, these teachers plan lessons, prepare tests, grade papers, prepare report cards, meet with parents, and supervise other activities. It is also often necessary for them to maintain classroom discipline. Secondary school teachers often meet individually with students to discuss homework assignments or academic or personal problems.

Teachers design classroom lessons to meet their students' needs and abilities. To explain a certain topic, they may lecture or use films, photographs, readings, and other techniques. Teachers always interact with the students and ask and answer questions to make sure the students understand the lessons. In order to reinforce the material learned in class, teachers will assign homework, give tests, and encourage other projects that help students develop an understanding of the material. For example, science teachers supervise laboratory projects where students work with microscopes and other equipment, and some vocational education teachers supervise students working with tools and building materials.

Some secondary school teachers are specially trained to work with students who have disabilities. Others work with very bright students who are able to understand advanced lessons.

A teacher's day usually begins about 8 A.M. and finishes after 3 P.M. Before classes start, teachers take attendance and make announcements during a homeroom period. In between classes, they often oversee study halls and supervise lunchroom activities. Teachers often use free time during the day to grade papers and keep records of each student's attendance and classroom progress. After classroom activities are over, teachers often attend school meetings or meet with parents or students. Teachers must also use this time to grade more papers and prepare the next day's lessons. Many teachers are involved with student projects that require after-school participation, like the school newspaper.

Education and training

Secondary school teachers should be knowledgeable in their subjects and able to communicate with and motivate students. They should have a genuine enthusiasm for working with young people and be interested in helping them learn. Teachers should also be able to present lessons in a creative way. Patience, understanding, and the ability to answer questions about schoolwork and other matters are very important.

The best way to become a teacher is to get a bachelor's or master's degree while completing an approved teacher training program. Many colleges and universities offer these programs in their education department. Students must take a number of courses in the subject they especially want to teach as well as a number of education courses covering teaching techniques and related subjects. Students must also spend several months teaching in a high school under the supervision of an experienced teacher. Upon completion of the program, students receive certification as secondary school teachers.

All teachers must be certified before beginning work, and many school systems require additional qualifications. While working, teachers must often attend education conferences and summer workshops to further their training.

▶ A secondary school teacher explains a science project to several students.

Earnings
The need for secondary school teachers should grow in the 1990s, but so should the number of people interested in pursuing a job in this field. Many people enjoy the challenge of working with students and the advantages of having summers off.

The average yearly salary for secondary school teachers in public schools is about $30,300. Those teaching in private schools often earn less. Many teachers have summer jobs to supplement their earnings.

Ways of getting more information
A good way to find out if you would enjoy being a teacher is to observe your own teachers at work. Most teachers will be happy to

discuss the advantages and disadvantages of the profession.

In addition, write to the following for more information:

▶ American Federation of Teachers
   555 New Jersey Avenue, NW
   Washington, DC 20001

▶ National Education Association
   1201 16th Street, NW
   Washington, DC 20036

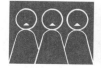

Secretaries

Other articles to look at:
► **Computer Operators**
► **Legal Assistants**
► **Medical Record Administrators**
► **Receptionists**
► **Typists**

What secretaries do

Secretaries help offices run smoothly. They handle correspondence, schedule appointments, do typing and word processing, take dictation, make travel arrangements, keep records and files, and take care of many other details that are so important to a well-organized place of business.

The duties of secretaries depend on a number of things: the kind of business that employs them, their own job training, and the number of other workers in the firm who can do special jobs. Special jobs might include writing in shorthand and using shorthand machines, working with computers, or dealing with foreign-language materials. Generally, secretaries employed in large firms do not do as many different jobs as those who work in smaller companies.

Many secretaries specialize in certain tasks and so have special titles, including *legal secretaries,* who prepare legal papers such as wills, leases, and court motions; *medical secretaries,* who must be familiar enough with medical terms to be able to transcribe them from tape recordings; and *technical secretar-*

ies, who work for engineers and scientists and help them prepare very technical articles and reports. These papers often include mathematics and graphics, which are very difficult to type into manuscript form.

Other kinds of secretaries include *social secretaries,* who work for celebrities or high-level executives and perform such duties as arranging dinners and social gatherings, keeping appointment schedules, and handling correspondence; *school secretaries,* who take care of the clerical duties at various kinds of schools; and *membership secretaries,* who work for associations or clubs, putting together membership lists and directories.

Education and training

Secretaries need a high school education and some advanced training as well. Some students take business education classes, which include typing, shorthand, and business English. They then either look for a job or go on to college. Employers prefer hiring students who have had some technical training after high school, especially in the use of computers. Still, most clerical workers receive some on-the-job training by the firm that hires them. Students can get good job experience by working part-time as file clerks, typists, or receptionists.

There are many similarities and differences among secretarial jobs. Every business has its own way of doing things. In general, secretaries need good reading, spelling, grammatical, and mathematical skills. Many com-

▶ Checking the original document against the entry on the computer, a secretary maintains a computer file system for her director.

panies give exams to job applicants that test these skills. Employers also look for speed, accuracy, and neatness. Careless mistakes are very costly for any business.

Earnings

The job outlook for secretaries is mixed. New computerized office equipment means that secretarial work will be done faster by fewer people. Still, companies are always looking for bright, enthusiastic secretaries.

Yearly salaries for secretaries range from about $18,000 to about $30,000, depending on skill, experience, and level of responsibility. Executive secretaries who have worked for a company for many years can earn $35,000 or more per year.

Ways of getting more information

For more information on secretarial careers, write to:

▶ Association of Independent Colleges and Schools
  1 Dupont Circle, NW, Suite 350
  Washington, DC 20036

▶ National Association of Legal Secretaries (International)
  2250 East 73rd Street, Suite 550
  Tulsa, OK 74136

Security Consultants

Other articles to look at:
- ▶ **Border Patrol Officers**
- ▶ **Forensic Experts**
- ▶ **Police Officers**
- ▶ **Private Investigators**
- ▶ **Security Guards**

What security consultants do

Security consultants are engaged in protective service work. Anywhere there are important people or valuable property and information, consultants may be called in to develop security plans as a means of protection. They are involved in preventing theft, vandalism, fraud, kidnapping, and other crimes.

Security consultants often work with companies to help them protect their equipment and records from unwanted intruders. A consultant will study the physical conditions of a facility and observe how a company conducts its operations before making any suggestions. The consultant will then discuss options with company officials. The amount of money that can be spent on security will greatly influence the security proposal. For example, a large company that produces military equipment may be advised to fence off its property and place electronic surveillance equipment at several points along the fence. The company may also be advised to install closed circuit television cameras and hire several security guards to monitor restricted areas. A smaller company that makes computers may be able to only install burglar alarms around specially restricted areas. A consultant will analyze all the possibilities and then present a written proposal to management for approval.

Consultants also oversee the installation of the equipment, make sure it is working properly, and then check frequently to make sure the client is satisfied. In the case of a crime, the consultant must investigate the cause of the problem (usually working with police officers and other security personnel) and then adapt the security system so that similar problems are not repeated.

Security consultants may also be called on to protect famous people from harm or from being kidnapped. These consultants accompany their clients on trips and conduct investigative checks on people who meet their clients.

Education and training

The work may involve a lot of travel, especially if the client is located in another city. Consultants should be in good physical condition because of the pressure involved in working on important projects, but great physical strength is not required.

The best way to become a security consultant is to combine several years of experience in crime prevention—either as a police officer or private investigator—with a college degree in business administration, criminal justice, or a similar field. Specific training in an area of specialization is also helpful. For example, if a consultant works closely with

▶ A security consultant explains the most appropriate security system and its cost to business clients.

nuclear power plants, he or she should have some previous work experience at a power plant and have a comprehensive knowledge of how these plants operate.

Earnings

As concerns for security continue to rise, consultants should find very good job opportunities in the 1990s.

Earnings vary greatly, depending on the consultant's training and experience. Those with a bachelor's degree can expect to earn $26,000 to $32,000 per year, while those with a master's degree should earn between $34,000 and $41,000 annually. Experienced consultants can earn over $50,000 a year.

Ways of getting more information

For more information write to:

▶ American Society for Industrial Security
1655 N. Fort Myer Drive, Suite 1200
Arlington, VA 22209

▶ International Association of Security Service
PO Box 8202
Northfield, IL 60093

Security Guards

Other articles to look at:
▶ **Bodyguards**
▶ **Border Patrol Officers**
▶ **Police Officers**
▶ **Security Consultants**
▶ **State Police Officers**

What security guards do

Security guards keep public and private property safe from theft, vandalism, fire, and illegal entry. Sports arenas, office buildings, banks, schools, hospitals, and stores are just a few of the places that security guards protect. For example, a bank guard will ensure that money is not stolen, and an office guard will stop certain people from entering the building.

Other names for the various kinds of security guards are *patroller, merchant patroller, bouncer, gate tender, armored-car guard,* and *airline security representative.* Most security guards wear uniforms. However, in situations where it is important for the guard to blend in with the general public, ordinary clothes are worn. Some security guards work during the day, while others are hired for night guard duty. A security guard might be assigned to one spot, such as at a doorway, to answer people's questions, give directions, or keep possible troublemakers away. Other guards make rounds, or regular tours, of a building or its surrounding land to make sure the property is safe and secure.

Security guards may sign visitors in and out of a building, direct traffic at a concert, enforce no-smoking rules, or inspect packages coming into a building. Often they carry two-way radios so they can communicate with other guards. Those who are likely to encounter criminal activity in their work may also carry guns. Security guards may work indoors or outdoors, day or night, and may be standing much of the time. They may have to work in bad weather and may sometimes face dangerous situations.

Guards often work alone, but they usually have contact with other people in the area they are watching. They are sometimes in contact with a central station away from their job area so that if they fail to send a certain signal, the central station will investigate further. Guards must always be alert for danger and threats.

Education and training

There are no special educational requirements for security guards. Most employers like to hire guards who have at least a high school education. A security guard should be healthy, alert, calm in emergencies, and able to follow directions. Good eyesight and hearing are important, too. People who have had military or police experience are often considered to be good candidates for security guard jobs. Some employers may ask applicants to take sight, hearing, or aptitude tests. For some security guard jobs, experience with firearms is required. Applicants for certain guard positions may have to pass a security check, assuring that they have never been guilty of a serious crime. Security guards who work for the federal government are required to have previous military service.

Earnings

There is expected to be a strong demand for security guards throughout the 1990s. This is partly because the crime rate is rising and partly because many security guards will be retiring. The turnover rate in this occupation is high, which means that many people are hired to replace those leaving or being dropped from jobs. There will be opportunities in full-time positions as well as for those who want part-time or second jobs at night or on weekends.

Security guards earn an average of $5.71 per hour. The average is higher for those who work in certain industries. For example, a guard at a manufacturing company could earn $10.00 an hour, whereas a person who is a guard in a department store might earn $6.50. The difference in wages also depends on the guard's experience. Security guards working for the federal government can earn a starting salary of $12,500 to $14,100 a year and can go on to earn a yearly average of about $16,300.

Ways of getting more information

Because of the experience required, young people ordinarily cannot get part-time jobs as security guards. However, they can perform similar duties as lifeguards, school monitors, and safety patrol workers.

▶ With several television monitors at his disposal, a security guard is able to see many areas at once.

For more information write to:

▶ Int'l. Security and Detective Alliance
PO Box 6303
Corpus Christi, TX 78466

▶ International Security Officers' Police and Guard Union
321 86th Street
Brooklyn, NY 11209

▶ International Union of Security Officers
2404 Merced Street
San Leandro, CA 94577

Semiconductor Technicians

Other articles to look at:
▶ **Computer-Service Technicians**
▶ **Electrical and Electronics Engineers**
▶ **Integrated Circuit Technicians**
▶ **Printed-Circuit-Board Technicians**

What semiconductor technicians do

Semiconductor technicians work in research laboratories, carrying out a variety of tasks to assist engineering staff in developing new designs for semiconductor chips. These tiny chips, often smaller than a fingernail, contain many miniaturized electronic circuits and components, and they are used in many kinds of modern machines.

Semiconductor chips, which are also called microchips, are made out of materials that have electrical properties somewhere between those of insulators and conductors. Because the circuits in chips are so small, the area of electronics concerned with chips and their circuitry is often called microelectronics. Therefore, semiconductor technicians are also called *microelectronics technicians*.

Semiconductor technicians work on making samples of new kinds of chips and on making limited numbers of chips that have been custom-designed for special purposes. To do this, they must have a broad knowledge of electronic theory, and they need to be familiar with the operating principles of the equipment in the laboratory where they work. They also must know about the specifications that their company has established for the products they will make.

Working under the direction of engineers, the technicians operate a variety of processing machines. Most of this equipment is highly complex and specialized. Using the machines, they convert layout designs for electronic circuitry to patterns that can be put on thin slices of semiconductor material called wafers. They clean, coat, bake, and etch the wafer surface and treat it in other ways. They put layers of different materials on certain areas of the surface. At various stages in the processing they test the wafers to verify that they have gotten the intended results. They cut the processed wafers into individual chips, then assemble and mount the chips into appropriate coverings.

Semiconductor technicians must also keep records about all the steps in the wafer processing operations and about the results of the tests they perform. They may assist engineers in analyzing this data and in preparing reports to describe and evaluate the new designs they have developed.

Education and training

Employers usually prefer to hire semiconductor technicians who have graduated from high school and who have finished a two-year training program such as those offered at junior and community colleges or technical institutes. A program in electrical engineering technology or electronics technology is probably the best preparation for work in this field. Because a semiconductor technician's job involves a range of duties, a training program should include a good theoretical foundation. It should also help the student develop skills in reading technical information and writing clear reports.

While in high school, students should take courses in algebra and geometry, physical sciences, computers, electrical shop, and English.

Earnings

Employment opportunities for new semiconductor technicians are not expected to be as good as in the past. Foreign competition in the semiconductor industry may hold back the level of production in the United States. However, the demand for microchips appears to be unlimited, because of their efficiency, speed, and low cost when used in many different kinds of machines.

The earnings of semiconductor technicians vary depending on their level of experience, geographical location, and their employer. In general, technicians make salaries in the $20,000 to $30,000 range, although some may earn more and a few less.

Ways of getting more information

Students who live in areas where there are companies that manufacture semiconductors may be able to arrange to talk with a technician working in a research and development department. Joining an electronics club or building electronics kits may provide some useful experience. By reading current magazines that cover microelectronics and computers, students can find out about the changes that are constantly going on in this industry.

▶ At several lab stations, semiconductor technicians carry out various phases of testing on semiconductors.

Students may also write to the following organizations for more information:

▶ Electronic Industries Association
  2001 Pennsylvania Avenue, NW, Suite 1100
  Washington, DC 20006-1813

▶ Electronic Industries Foundation
  1901 Pennsylvania Avenue, NW, Suite 700
  Washington, DC 20006

▶ Electronics Technicians Association, International
  602 North Jackson Street
  Greencastle, IN 46135

Service Station Attendants

Other articles to look at:
▶ **Automobile Mechanics**
▶ **Automotive Engine Technicians**
▶ **Diesel Mechanics**
▶ **Motorcycle Mechanics**
▶ **Petroleum Drilling Occupations**

What service station attendants do

Service station attendants provide all kinds of services for the customers who drive into the gas stations where they work. They pump gas, clean windshields, and check water levels in radiators and batteries, oil levels in engines, and air pressure in tires. They may sell tires, batteries, light bulbs, and other parts; install accessories like windshield wipers, rearview mirrors, and spark plugs; and do minor repair and maintenance work—such as fixing flat tires, replacing mufflers, rotating tires, and adding oil, water, and air as needed. Service station attendants may perform these services on cars, buses, trucks, and other vehicles.

Service station attendants often provide directions to motorists who are lost. Some drive tow trucks to stranded motorists; others offer car washes along with gas tank fillups. In some stations attendants are responsible for keeping service areas and restrooms clean, for setting up displays, and for taking inventory of station supplies. In other self-service stations, attendants may only accept payment for fuel sold.

At some gas stations there is also a small store that sells items such as newspapers, milk, and food items. Service station attendants who are employed in such places often must work the cash register and take care of the rest of the store. Wherever they work, service station attendants must enjoy working both with cars and with the public, and must not mind the grease, grime, and long hours that go along with the job.

Education and training

It is possible to become a service station attendant without completing high school, but most employers prefer high school graduates. Though applicants are generally trained on the job, some large oil companies have their own training programs that range from two weeks to two months—and for these programs a high school diploma is required.

Training programs for service station attendants are also available through the distributive education programs available in many high schools. People interested in becoming mechanic-attendants should look into the programs with an emphasis on mechanics conducted by vocational education agencies and local offices of the U.S. Employment Service.

With experience and, in some cases, additional training, service station attendants can go on to become mechanics, station managers, or oil company salespersons. Many of the most ambitious and competent attendants eventually go on to lease a station from an oil company or buy their own service station.

Earnings

Jobs for service station attendants will grow slowly throughout the 1990s. This is because fewer and fewer gas stations are offering vehicle repair and maintenance and are merely selling gasoline and other items. Most attendants are needed only in self-service gas stations, to accept payment for the gas that customers pump themselves. However, more attendants may be needed to service the complex new pollution control devices on new cars.

Wages for service station attendants vary depending on the size, nature, and location of the service stations for which they work. Salaries are not high, however, with the majority of attendants earning an average of about $275 per week. Some, however, can earn up to about $510 per week.

Ways of getting more information

Interested students can help parents pump gas at self-service stations and can learn such routine maintenance tasks as changing oil, replacing windshield wipers, and fixing flat tires. Talk to the attendants at your local gas station for a firsthand account of what the job is like.

For more information on working as a service station attendant, write to:

▶ American Petroleum Institute
  1220 L Street, NW
  Washington, DC 20005

▶ Service Station Dealers of America
  499 South Capital Street, NW
  Washington, DC 20003-4013

▶ A service station attendant pumps gas for a customer.

Services Sales Representatives

Other articles to look at:
► **Door-to-Door Sales Workers**
► **Manufacturers' Sales Representatives**
► **Real Estate Agents and Brokers**
► **Stockbrokers**
► **Telemarketers**

What services sales representatives do

When we think of salespeople we often think only of people selling such things as books, clothing, and cars. But things that people do for each other are also sold, things like telephone repair, detective work, and dry cleaning services. *Services sales representatives* may work for any company that has services to sell. They may sell printing, advertising, cable television, and linen supply services. These sales representatives, called sales reps for short, may also work for companies selling educational, computer and data processing, burial, shipping, car repair, and hotel services. For example, hotel sales representatives call government, business, and social groups to book rooms for visits and conferences. Sales reps that are called *fundraisers* plan programs to raise money for charities and other causes, such as the Special Olympics for handicapped children and adults.

The services that individual sales representatives sell may be very different, but the methods they use have much in common. First, they learn as much as they can about the services offered by their company. Then, they make lists of possible customers. To do so, they use business and telephone directories. They ask current customers for the names of others who might be interested in their company's services.

There are also organizations that sell lists of businesses and individuals to representatives. Credit card companies regularly sell their list of cardholders.

After identifying possible customers, sales workers meet with them and explain how their company's services can meet their needs. They answer any questions the customers may have and try to convince them to buy their company's services.

Services sales reps may not immediately make a sale. They may make more than one visit and may call and send letters to the customer. Once a sale has been made, these workers visit the customer to make sure that the services have met their needs. They also find out if more services are needed by their customers.

Keeping customers satisfied is an important part of this job. Services sales representatives get many of their new customers through their current ones. Also, when customers are happy, they usually continue to buy the company's services.

Selling can be stressful work. Sales reps who are assigned large territories may spend a lot of time traveling, sometimes even weeks at a time. Appointments are usually scheduled for a time most convenient for the customer.

Education and training

Many employers prefer workers with a college degree in a field related to the services being sold. For example, companies that sell computer services may look for workers with a degree in computer science. Those that sell advertising services may want workers with a degree in advertising. Job seekers with only a high school diploma may be hired if they have a proven sales record.

Many companies have training programs for their sales representatives. Workers learn about the company's services and about various sales methods. They may also attend special training sessions given by technical schools, colleges, and universities.

Earnings

The job outlook for services sales representatives is quite good for the 1990s. This is because of the rapid increase in demand for services. Many representatives do not stay in their jobs for a long time. As these workers leave their jobs, more openings are created.

In the early 1990s, services sales workers had average annual earnings of between $22,000 and $25,000. Some experienced workers earn more than $100,000 per year. Most sales representatives receive a salary as well as commissions (a percentage of the amount of sales they make). Some are paid only a salary; others work for commissions only. Some companies offer prizes and bonuses for workers who go beyond the company's sales goals.

Ways of getting more information

For more information about a career as a services sales representative write to the following:

▶ Maintaining contact with customers, a services sales representative meets with clients regularly to make sure that her service is working well.

▶ Sales and Marketing Executives International
  Statler Office Tower, Suite 458
  Cleveland, OH 44115

▶ Service Business Marketing Association
  PO Box 909
  Buena Vista, CO 81211

Sheet-Metal Workers

Other articles to look at:
▶ **Automobile-Body Repairers**
▶ **Construction Workers**
▶ **Heating and Cooling Mechanics**
▶ **Plumbers**
▶ **Roofers**

What sheet-metal workers do

Sheet-metal workers make, install, and repair rain gutters, outdoor signs, and other articles of light sheet-metal, including air-conditioning, heating, and ventilation duct systems. (Ducts are the long, metal tubes in buildings that carry hot and cold air or water.) Workers cut, bend, shape, and fasten the sheet-metal to form the desired object. Sheet-metal workers are often employed to work on homes and other types of construction projects.

When making an object, sheet-metal workers first determine the size and type of sheet-metal to use. Working from blueprints, drawings, or instructions from supervisors, they determine the measurements and angles of the object to be made. They then lay out the sheet-metal and mark the pattern to be cut. In many shops, workers use computerized measuring equipment to lay out the pattern so that the least amount of metal is wasted when the pattern is cut. In shops without this equipment, workers use tapes, rulers, and other devices to make the measurements. Workers then use machine tools to cut the objects.

Sheet-metal workers do not make ducts or other objects from one piece of material.

Rather, they measure and cut a number of metal pieces and then join them together to form larger sections of the finished product. Before the many pieces are joined together, workers must inspect each piece to make sure it is made correctly. They then drill or punch holes into the metal and assemble the parts by welding or fastening them together.

At the construction site, workers install ducts, pipes, and other objects by joining the various parts together and securing the sections in the correct location. Workers may use hammers, pliers, or other tools to make adjustments to the objects or make some parts by hand.

Education and training

Sheet-metal workers should be able to read blueprints and sketches and carefully follow instructions. They must be good at working with sheet-metal and using the proper methods for fastening metal pieces together. Workers need to be skillful in using hand tools, power tools, and measuring devices.

The work involves a great deal of minor physical exertion such as kneeling, reaching, bending, and stretching. In addition, the job may be physically demanding, requiring the lifting of heavy pieces of sheet-metal.

The best way to become a sheet-metal worker is to complete a four- or five-year apprenticeship program, which includes on-the-job training and classroom instruction. While under the supervision of experienced workers, apprentices learn to measure, cut, and install sheet-metal articles. In the classroom, apprentices learn how to lay out sheet-metal and read blueprints. Most apprentices are high school graduates.

Some people become sheet-metal workers without going through an apprenticeship program. They acquire their skills informally by working as helpers while they learn. Helpers begin with simple tasks and gradually take on more difficult assignments.

Earnings

With an expected increase in construction and the need to continually repair or replace duct systems, there should be good job opportunities in the 1990s. Some workers may experience brief periods of unemployment if there is a slowdown in new construction.

The average annual salary for sheet-metal workers is about $39,000 per year. Apprentices start off making about half this amount, but their pay is periodically increased, so that they are making nearly this amount by the end of their apprenticeship.

Ways of getting more information

A good way to find out about being a sheet-metal worker is to take shop courses. It is also possible to interview sheet-metal workers and in that way learn more about the profession.

In addition, write to the following organizations and ask for information about being a sheet-metal worker:

▶ A sheet-metal worker attaches a ring of metal to a cylinder.

▶ Associated Builders and Contractors
   729 15th Street, NW
   Washington, DC 20005

▶ Sheet Metal and Air Conditioning
   Contractors' National Association
   PO Box 221230
   Chantilly, VA 22022-1230

Shoe Industry Workers

Other articles to look at:
► **Furniture Manufacturing Workers**
► **Leather Tanning and Finishing Workers**
► **Shoe Repairers**
► **Textile Workers**

What shoe industry workers do

According to recent statistics the average American buys four or five pairs of shoes each year. These shoes are produced by workers in factories who operate more than 300 different machines.

Cutters arrange dies on leather hides. A die-cutting machine then stamps out the parts for several matching pairs of shoes. *Stock handlers* take these cut parts to a fitting room where *fitting room workers* make the upper parts of the shoes. They use machines to punch holes in the uppers, trim cloth linings, taper edges, put in eyelets and buckles, and lace the shoes.

Meanwhile, workers in sole rooms are preparing insoles, outsoles, and heels. Workers take these parts to last rooms. A *last* is a wooden or plastic form shaped like a foot. Workers called *last assemblers* put the upper and lower parts of a shoe on a last, and then run machines that join the parts together.

The next stop is the bottoming department, where workers attach steel or wooden shanks and outsoles to the shoes. The shoes are then removed from the lasts and sent to the finishing department.

Workers in the finishing department put heels on the shoes and trim the outsoles. They also cement cloth linings and inner heel pads in place. *Tree department workers* clean, finish, and polish the upper parts of the shoes. Finally, *packers* pack the shoes for storing or shipping.

Education and training

Although a high school education is not required for consideration as a shoe industry worker, applicants with a diploma are likely to be hired before those who have not graduated. High school courses that would be helpful include shop and sewing courses. Some technical schools offer courses in shoemaking. Students who complete such courses will probably start at a higher wage than those with no training.

Most shoe industry workers learn their skills on the job. It may take from six months to two years for workers to become highly skilled at their jobs.

Earnings

The employment opportunities for shoe industry workers in the 1990s should be slower than average. More and more shoes are now imported from foreign countries, decreasing the need for workers in the United States.

Most shoe industry workers are paid by piecework rates. This means they get paid according to how much they produce. In the early 1990s the average pay for shoe industry

▶ Shaping the upper section of a leather shoe, a shoe industry worker prepares the shoe for sewing.

workers was about $6.00 to $11.00 per hour. The highest paid shoe industry workers are cutters, who average about $17,000 per year.

New workers usually start at the prevailing minimum wage. After they learn their skill they can work quickly enough to be paid a piecework rate.

Ways of getting more information

For more information about a career as a shoe industry worker, write to the following:

▶ Shoe Service Institute of America
   5024-R Campbell Boulevard
   Baltimore, MD 21236

▶ Brotherhood of Shoe and Allied Craftsmen
   PO Box 390
   East Bridgewater, MA 02333

Shoe Repairers

Other articles to look at:
▶ **Knit Goods Industry Workers**
▶ **Leather Tanning and Finishing Workers**
▶ **Shoe Industry Workers**
▶ **Textile Workers**

What shoe repairers do

Shoe repairers fix shoes, most often heels and soles, and they also work on such other leather products as purses, luggage, saddles, and harnesses. Some workers, often called *custom shoemakers,* design and make special orthopedic shoes, which are prescribed by foot doctors for persons with medical problems.

Most shoe repairers work in small shops where they perform the whole range of jobs, such as sewing, trimming, dying, polishing, and so on. Many other shoemakers own their shops and so must combine the skills of a small business person with those of a shoemaker. Besides fixing shoes, those workers make estimates of repair costs, write up sales slips, do basic bookkeeping and accounting, and often supervise other employees.

Shoe repairers may start out working with a small kit, cleaning, polishing, and doing minor repairs on leather in locations where business workers are likely to be found. Airports, bus stations, train stations, and other areas where people may have some spare time for getting their shoes fixed and polished are the most practical locations for shoe repairers.

A good shoe repairer must have the ability to work with precision and skill on small areas. In order to restitch a shoe, the worker should be able to either run a sewing machine or hand stitch an area along the same path it was originally sewn. Replacing worn soles or heels needs to be done so that the wearer can still feel comfortable in the shoes.

Dying shoes requires knowledge of dyes and how leather responds to the dyes. To match a dress color, the shoe repairer needs to know how dark the leather will get from the dye. Experience and testing are the most effective ways to learn the trade.

Working with specific leather items such as saddles may be done by people who choose to specialize in the crafting of one product, but since leather is used, any shoe repairer can add those items to his or her list of crafts. Purses, gloves, saddles, and other sewn leather products may require repair or restitching, and if a shoe repairer is qualified to work on those things, it will increase the amount of business done.

Education and training

There are no special requirements for becoming a shoe repair worker, although a high school diploma or vocational school training is helpful. Training programs are offered by the U.S. Manpower Development and Training Act.

These workers should have good hand-to-eye coordination and good eyesight. Working as an apprentice and studying under someone

▶ A shoe repairer cuts a piece of leather to put on a shoe.

who has experience is the best way to learn the trade.

Earnings

The demand for shoe repair workers will be decreasing somewhat in the 1990s as more people wear shoes that don't need repair work—athletic shoes, for example. Leather is still a popular material, however, and mending should be in demand for some time to come.

The average pay for shoe repair workers is between $8.00 and $11.00 per hour, with shop owners earning quite a bit more. Beginning workers earn about $6.00 per hour.

Ways of getting more information
For more information write to:

▶ Shoe Service Institute of America
  5024-R Campbell Boulevard
  Baltimore, MD 21236

▶ Leather Industries of America
  1000 Thomas Jefferson Street, NW,
  Suite 515
  Washington, DC 20007

Silverware Industry Workers

Other articles to look at:
► **Electroplating Workers**
► **Forge Shop Workers**
► **Glass Manufacturing Workers**
► **Jewelers**
► **Tool and Die Makers**

What silverware industry workers do

Silverware industry workers design and manufacture flatware and hollowware. Eating utensils such as forks, knives, and spoons are known as flatware. Containers such as pitchers, sugar bowls, and cups are known as hollowware. Flatware and hollowware can be made of a variety of materials. These include sterling silver, pewter, and stainless steel. Some flatware is plated, which means it has a coating of silver or gold over another metal. Hollowware may also be plated.

Silverware designers design the flatware and hollowware. They make drawings of the pieces as well as the patterns (if any) that will go on them. After a design has been approved, *modelers* use clay or plaster to make a mold of the piece. This model is used by *tool and die makers* to make steel dies of the piece. Dies are a type of tool used in cutting, shaping, and stamping the metal. Next, sheets of metal are fed into machines that cut them into flat shapes. These shapes are then formed and rounded by other machines. The extra metal is trimmed away by workers called *trimmers*. Rough edges are smoothed on a belt. Workers stamp designs on the handles of pieces. To do so, they use dies and a drop hammer, which is a hammer that is mechanically raised and dropped to make marks on the material. The pieces are then washed and polished.

The spouts, handles, and other parts of plated hollowware are made by pouring melted metal into molds. *Silverware assemblers* attach these parts to teapots, cream pitchers, and other types of hollowware. To do so, they use solder or another type of adhesive (glue). Then the pieces are plated with silver, gold, or a mixture of metals. This is the job of *electroplaters*. *Oxidizers* place a solution on silver or silver-plated pieces. This solution makes the design stand out after the piece has been buffed.

Most silverware industry workers are employed by factories located in New England. Factories are also found in the state of New York and in other areas of the country.

Education and training

An associate's or bachelor's degree in design is usually needed to become a silverware designer. Skilled workers in this field must complete an apprenticeship program. These programs combine classroom work with on-the-job training. Workers who have completed technical school programs in related fields are in demand in this industry. Even those applying for unskilled jobs should have a high school diploma, if possible.

▶ A silverware industry worker checks the curve of spoon handles against the original model.

Earnings

The job outlook for silverware industry workers is not very good. More and more of the silverware being sold in the United States is imported from other countries, and the high price of silver and steel has also had an effect on this industry. Most job openings will occur as workers switch to other fields or retire. Few new jobs will be created.

Salaries of silverware designers range from $15,000 per year to more than $20,000. Skilled workers who get paid by the piece may make more than $9.00 per hour. Unskilled workers start at about $5.50 to $7.00 per hour. Tool and die makers can earn as much as $12.00 per hour.

Ways of getting more information

For more information about careers in the silverware industry write to the following:

▶ Manufacturing Jewelers and Silversmiths of America
   100 India Street
   Providence, RI 02903-4313

▶ Sterling Silversmiths Guild of America
   312-A Wyndhurst Avenue
   Baltimore, MD 21210

Singers

Other articles to look at:
- ▶ **Actors and Actresses**
- ▶ **Dancers**
- ▶ **Music Teachers**
- ▶ **Musicians**

What singers do

Singers are musicians whose instruments are their voices. They use their knowledge of musical tone, phrasing, harmony, and melody to create vocal music.

Singers are classified in two ways. The first way is by the range of their voices. Sopranos have the highest voices, followed by contraltos, tenors, altos, and basses, who have the lowest voices. The second way that singers may be classified is by the type of music they sing—including rock, folk, opera, jazz, or country.

Nearly all singers work with instrumental musicians. A singer's backup group may be as small as one piano player or a single guitarist or as large as a full symphony orchestra. In between are jazz combos, dance bands, rock bands, and so on.

Many singers travel throughout the country and even the world bringing their music to appreciative audiences. A jazz singer, for example, may play to audiences in small clubs in cities across the United States. An opera singer, by comparison, may sing in huge opera houses in the Americas, Europe, and on other continents.

Some singers are primarily studio singers. That is, they rarely perform in front of audiences but instead record their singing in sound studios. They may record television and radio commercials, jingles, and the like. Most singers, though, must be able to perform in front of an audience.

Singers can also be actors. Musical plays on the stage require singers with strong voices who can also act well. Many singers have made their careers in such plays.

Since young singers need vocal training, many experienced singers choose to be teachers. Just as piano teachers help their students to master the keyboard, singing teachers help their students to master their vocal talents. Singing teachers help students learn to read music, develop their voices, and breathe correctly.

Education and training

Most singers begin learning their skill at an early age. Young children may be part of school or church choirs. In high school, students may join concert choirs or take part in musical plays that include extensive vocal training. Usually, students must audition for enrollment in these programs.

In addition to formal schooling, many singers enlist the aid of singing teachers and voice coaches. These teachers help their students to refine their vocal talents. No amount of training, however, can substitute for talent, dedication, and drive. Singers must be truly devoted to their art to succeed.

▶ A cast of singers performs an operetta on stage.

Earnings

There always has been strong competition for the limited number of job opportunities for singers. Usually only the most talented will find regular employment.

Singers' wages vary so widely that it is difficult to give a true indication of a vocalist's earning power. Singers who become famous, whether in popular or classical performance, can expect to earn a good deal of money. Many studio singers also earn good wages. Some singers, however, must work at other jobs to gain additional money.

Ways of getting more information

For more information about a career as a singer write to the following:

▶ American Federation of Musicians of the U.S. and Canada
  Paramount Building
  1501 Broadway, Suite 600
  New York, NY 10036

▶ American Guild of Musical Artists
  1727 Broadway
  New York, NY 10019

▶ National Association of Schools of Music
  11250 Roger Bacon Drive, No. 21
  Reston, Va 22090

Ski Lift Operators

Other articles to look at:
- ▶ **Electrical Repairers**
- ▶ **Operating Engineers**
- ▶ **Recreation Workers**
- ▶ **Structural-Steel Workers**

What ski lift operators do
Ski lift operators maintain and run the lifts that carry skiers to the top of a slope. There are several types of ski lifts. With a rope tow, skiers grasp a motor-driven rope and are pulled uphill. The chair lift features a series of chairs that hang from a moving cable. Skiers sit on the chairs and are transported uphill. Gondolas and tram lifts operate like a chair lift but have enclosed cars to carry skiers to the top of the slope. Although ski lift operators maintain and operate all types of ski lifts, most work with chair lifts.

Ski lift operators work in resorts that feature downhill skiing. Operators must check the loading area around the ski lift to make sure it is clear of all freshly fallen snow, ice, or other material. The loading platform must be clear to allow skiers to get on and off as safely as possible. Operators then check the electrical equipment that powers the lift. They inspect the engine and observe the brakes, gearbox, and other parts. Operators might make minor adjustments to the equipment, but any major repairs are referred to the maintenance staff. The operators then turn on the ski lift and test it by having one of the operators ride the lift to the top of the slope. This operator must check the connecting cables and other equipment along the way. The brakes are also tested. Again, any repair problems are referred to the maintenance staff.

Throughout the day, operators at the bottom of the slope help skiers onto the lift while those at the top help skiers off of the lift. If someone is not seated properly or has trouble getting on or off the lift, the operator stops the lift until the problem is resolved.

Education and training
Ski lift operators usually have at least a high school diploma and some skiing experience. The skiing background helps operators relate to other skiers and makes them aware of possible problems skiers might have with the lifts. Many operators have at least some college training, and often operators are college students who are working part-time or taking time off from school.

All beginning ski lift operators are given on-the-job training under the supervision of experienced operators. New operators are shown how to maintain and run the equipment and how to help skiers in the most effective manner.

Earnings
Skiing and other outdoor sports are gaining in popularity and this should lead to good job opportunities in the 1990s for ski lift operators.

▶ A ski lift operator guides skiers onto the chair lift.

Ski lift operators only work during the winter months, and each year there are many openings to replace those who do not return from the previous season.

The average salary is about $8.00 an hour. Because the job is part-time, most operators do not receive health insurance, vacation, or other benefits.

Ways of getting more information

A good way to find out if you would enjoy being a ski lift operator is to visit a ski resort and talk to an operator. It might also be possible to get a part-time job as an operator's helper and in that way learn more about the profession.

In addition, write to the following organization and ask for information about being a ski lift operator:

▶ United States Ski Association
PO Box 100
Park City, UT 84060

Social Workers

Other articles to look at:
▶ **Career Counselors**
▶ **Guidance Counselors**
▶ **Human Services Workers**
▶ **Psychologists**
▶ **Sociologists**

What social workers do

Social workers work with people to ease personal and community problems caused by such things as poverty, homelessness, unemployment, illness, broken homes, family discord, and physical, mental, and emotional handicaps. Employed by public and private agencies, social workers do their job through individual casework, group work, or community organizations.

With casework, the social worker, or *caseworker,* meets face-to-face with the troubled individual or family. These caseworkers may work in schools, for example, to help students who skip school or have other behavior problems. They may work in hospitals, helping sick people and their families adjust to the special problems caused by their illnesses. They may work in courts, police departments, and prison systems, counseling convicts, helping juvenile offenders, or assisting soon-to-be released prisoners return to life outside the jail. Some caseworkers are employed by adoption agencies; some work in drug and alcohol abuse programs; some work privately to help families find solutions to financial, emotional, or medical problems. Whether they meet in their own offices, in the clients' homes, or in official settings like schools and hospitals, caseworkers do their best to help clients resolve whatever problems are troubling them.

Group workers may be employed by community centers, settlement houses, youth organizations, institutions for children or the aged, hospitals, prisons, or housing projects. They provide both rehabilitation and recreational activities for groups of people with similar handicaps or problems. Group workers might help migrant workers adjust to their temporary surroundings. They might hold workshops for parents of diabetic children or for the children themselves. They also might work in nursing homes, planning social and recreational activities for the elderly. They often provide the same kinds of services that individual caseworkers provide, only on a group basis.

Community organization workers try to analyze the problems of an entire community and try to discover ways to solve them. Juvenile delinquency is one problem that might require total community cooperation for solution; high unemployment or crime rates are other such problems.

Being a social worker can sometimes be very emotional because the job requires paying so much attention to problems and needs in our society. Those who work for agencies that are understaffed, meaning that they do not have enough employees, can be under extra pressure.

Education and training

Social workers must be sensitive to people's problems and be able to handle them with a concerned, caring attitude, even if the problems make the worker sad or angry. They have to be able to accept responsibility and to try to solve problems even if they are under pressure.

A social worker needs at least a bachelor's degree in social work from an approved four-year college or university. Jobs with the most rewards and responsibilities go to applicants with a master's degree. A doctorate is required for some teaching, research, and supervisory jobs.

Earnings

Employment opportunities for social workers are expected to be good through the year 2000. This is because of the increasing needs of our growing and aging population. Most job opportunities will probably be a result of the need to replace those workers who leave the profession. As always, workers with the best education and most experience will win the best jobs.

Beginning earnings for full-time social workers with a bachelor's degree are about $20,000 per year. Beginning workers with a master's degree earn about $25,000 per year. Workers with advanced degrees and experience in a special area of expertise, such as administrators, can earn about $45,000 per year. Earnings also depend very much on the worker's experience and the type of agency one works for.

Ways of getting more information

Your library will have plenty of reading material on the history and nature of social work. You can also contact a local social agency, hospital, or community organization that uses social workers in its programs. Volunteering

▶ In a conference with clients, a social worker discusses the ways to handle the clients' problems.

as a junior counselor at a day camp will also offer opportunities to see what working with different sorts of people is like.

For more information write to:

▶ Council on Social Work Education
1600 Duke Street
Alexandria, VA 22314

▶ National Association of Social Workers
7981 Eastern Avenue
Silver Spring, MD 20910

Sociologists

Other articles to look at:
► **Anthropologists**
► **College and University Faculty**
► **Economists**
► **Political Scientists**
► **Psychologists**

What sociologists do

Sociologists study the various groups that human beings form. They study families, tribes, communities, and other social and political groups to understand how they develop and operate. To study these groups, sociologists observe them and record what they find. Besides observing groups themselves, sociologists may use population counts, historical documents, questionnaires, and tests. Lawmakers, educators, and others then use this information to help solve social problems.

A sociologist can specialize in any of several fields. *Criminologists* study causes of crime and ways to prevent it. *Urban sociologists* study cities and the ways people live within them. *Industrial sociologists* specialize in the relationships between employees in companies. *Clinical sociologists* study groups that do not work well or are poorly organized, and they help find ways to improve them. *Social ecologists* learn about how the environment affects where and how people live. These are just a few of the many areas in which sociologists may choose to work.

Sociologists often work closely with other social scientists and scientific professionals. For instance, statisticians help to organize the information they collect into mathematical formulas. They also work with psychologists, cultural anthropologists, economists, and political scientists.

Over two-thirds of all sociologists teach in colleges and universities. They may be working on sociology research projects at the same time. Other sociologists work for government agencies that deal with poverty, crime, community development, and similar social problems.

Education and training

With a bachelor's degree in sociology, a person can perhaps get a job doing interviews or collecting data. With a teaching certificate, he or she can teach sociology in a high school. Those with master's degrees can find jobs with research institutes, industries, or government agencies. It is important to note, however, that more than half of all working sociologists have a doctorate degree. Most of them teach in colleges and universities while doing their research. Helpful high school courses include English, foreign languages, mathematics, sciences, social studies, and other college preparatory courses.

Sociologists who wish to work for the federal government may be required to take a civil service examination. Those who want to work overseas may have to take a foreign-language proficiency test. Some clinical sociologists have to be certified by the Clinical Sociology Association (CSA). This requires a

► Sociologists discuss their findings from a group study.

doctoral degree, one year's experience as a clinical sociologist, and other proof of knowledge and skills.

Earnings

Job opportunities for sociologists in the 1990s will increase more slowly than average. The best jobs will go to those with doctoral degrees, while people with a master's degree will find themselves in stiff competition for jobs.

For sociologists who work for the federal government, those with a bachelor's degree can earn an average of about $15,800 to $19,400 per year in an entry-level position, depending on the worker's academic record. The starting salary for those with a master's degree is about $23,900. For doctorates, the average annual starting salary is around $28,900, although some start as high as $34,600.

The average salary level for sociologists working in industries is about $41,200, and for those in universities it is very similar.

Ways of getting more information

For more information, write:

► American Sociological Association
  1722 N Street, NW
  Washington, DC 20036

► Sociological Practice Association
  RD 2, Box 141A
  Chester, NY 10918

39

Soil-Conservation Technicians

Other articles to look at:
▶ **Agricultural Engineers**
▶ **Agricultural Scientists**
▶ **Farmers**
▶ **Foresters**
▶ **Forestry Technicians**

What soil-conservation technicians do

Soil-conservation technicians help land users to develop plans to use the soil wisely. They show farmers how to rotate their crops so that the nutrients in the soil are not exhausted. They also help foresters plan growth and harvesting cycles so that trees are not cut down before they mature.

Soil-conservation technicians perform a variety of duties. They assist engineers in surveying land. They plan tile drainage systems and irrigation systems. Soil-conservation technicians also make maps from aerial photographs and inspect specific areas to determine what conservation methods are needed.

Experienced soil-conservation technicians have specific titles and jobs. *Cartographic technicians* are responsible for charting or mapping areas of the earth. They also create charts that show specific geographic information. *Geodetic technicians* help to analyze, evaluate, compute, and select geodetic data—information that relates to the size, shape, and gravity of the earth. *Engineering technicians* test engineering materials for performance and efficiency and write reports on their findings.

Meteorological technicians analyze or predict weather and its effect on the earth's surface and on the activities of people. *Physical science technicians* assist professional scientists in adjusting and operating measuring instruments, mixing solutions, making routine chemical analyses, and setting up and operating testing equipment.

Surveying technicians make surveys for mapping and measuring purposes. They gather data for the design of highways and dams or for the creating of topographic maps and nautical and aeronautical charts. *Range conservationists* administer range conservation programs that enable people in the livestock industry to operate their ranges more efficiently and productively.

Education and training

A high school diploma is essential for anyone wishing to become a soil-conservation technician. High school students should take courses in mathematics, speech, writing, chemistry, and biology. Courses in vocational agriculture, which is the study of farming as an occupation, are also helpful.

After high school, students should enroll in a technical institute or a junior or community college that offers an associate degree in soil conservation. First-year courses in these programs include basic soils, chemistry, botany, zoology, and introduction to range management. Second-year courses include surveying, forestry, game management, fish management, and soil and water conservation.

▶ On a field that was once mined for coal, a soil-conservation technician studies the health of a wheat crop.

Earnings

Most soil-conservation technicians are employed by the federal government, and many others work for private owners of land. Employment opportunities are expected to be fair during the 1990s, because of the continuing need for environmental protection and water quality maintenance.

Technicians who work for the federal government can earn an average yearly salary of about $30,000. Those with doctorate degrees or in research jobs can earn a starting salary of as much as $34,600 each year. Salaries in private industry are usually lower.

Ways of getting more information

For more information about a career as a soil-conservation technician, contact:

▶ American Society of Agronomy
   677 South Segoe Road
   Madison, WI 53711

▶ Soil and Water Conservation Society
   7515 Northeast Ankeny Road
   Ankeny, IA 50021

Soil Scientists

Other articles to look at:
- ► **Agricultural Scientists**
- ► **Chemists**
- ► **Farmers**
- ► **Landscape Architects**
- ► **Soil-Conservation Technicians**

What soil scientists do

Soil is one of our most important natural resources. It provides the nutrients necessary to grow food for millions of people. To use soil wisely and keep it from washing away or otherwise being damaged, experts are needed to analyze it and determine the best ways to manage it. *Soil scientists* are these experts. They collect soil samples and study their chemical and physical characteristics. They study how soil responds to fertilizers and other farming practices in order to help farmers decide what types of crops to grow on certain soils.

Soil scientists do much of their work outdoors. They go to fields to take soil samples, and they spend many hours meeting with farmers and discussing ways of avoiding soil damage. A soil scientist may suggest that a farmer grow crops on different parts of a farm every several years so that the unused soil can replenish itself. The soil scientist may also recommend that a farmer use various fertilizers to put nutrients back into the soil or suggest ways of covering crops to keep the wind from blowing the soil away.

Soil scientists work for agricultural research laboratories, crop production companies, and other organizations. Although they usually answer agricultural questions, these scientists also work with road departments to advise them about the quality and condition of the soil over which roads will be built.

Some soil scientists travel to foreign countries to conduct research and observe the way other scientists treat the soil. Many are also involved with teaching at colleges, universities, and agricultural schools.

Education and training

Soil scientists should have a solid background in mathematics and science, particularly the physical and earth sciences. They should also be curious, be able to solve complex problems, and have good communication skills.

The best way to become a soil scientist is to get a master's degree in agricultural science. A degree in biology, physics, or chemistry might also be sufficient, but some course work in agriculture is highly desirable. A bachelor's degree in agricultural science may be adequate for some nonresearch jobs, but advancement opportunities will be limited. Many research and teaching positions require a doctorate.

High school students should take four years of mathematics and courses in earth science, physics, and chemistry. Classes in English and history are also recommended.

▶ A soil scientist tests the ground for water levels to see if there is enough water present for the plants.

Earnings

With agricultural concerns continuing to be an important issue in the coming years, soil scientists should have good job opportunities. There haven't been as many agricultural students as usual in the past few years, so schools will probably be optimistic about placing new graduates in jobs. Many of the openings will be with private companies; the government may not be hiring many new scientists.

For soil scientists in government jobs, the average yearly salary is about $37,000. Wages depend on one's educational degree, academic record, and years of experience.

Ways of getting more information

For more information, write to the following organizations:

▶ Soil and Water Conservation Society
  7515 Northeast Ankeny Road
  Ankeny, IA 50021

▶ Soil Science Society of America
  677 South Segoe Road
  Madison, WI 53711

Sound-Recording Technicians

Other articles to look at:
- ▶ **Audio-Control Technicians**
- ▶ **Broadcast Technicians**
- ▶ **Sound Technicians**
- ▶ **Studio Technicians**
- ▶ **Video Technicians**

What sound-recording technicians do

Sound-recording technicians are at the heart of any broadcast operation. These technicians, also known as *recording engineers,* are responsible for the quality of the sound that listeners hear, and so they operate and maintain video and sound-recording equipment. They record radio broadcasts and the sound portions of television programs and videotapes. Sometimes these technicians are responsible for operating equipment that is designed to produce special sound effects, like cars crashing and storms howling. Sound-recording technicians are also needed to record the sound portion of videos that businesses use to train their employees.

Some sound-recording technicians work in recording studios. They record the sound for musical, spoken, and dramatic phonograph records, tapes, and compact discs. To do so, the technician must be familiar with recording equipment, which involves the following: blank discs for vinyl mastering, multi-track tapes for cassettes and compact discs (CDs), and prerecorded sound. They record the sound that is needed for the production, record voices and instruments, then combine all the sounds onto one master tape. This tape is known as the mixed master.

While recording any sound, it is the primary task of the sound-recording technician to make sure the sound is right and that there is no unwanted noise coming through; they adjust volume, tone, and speed controls. To do this effectively they must understand how microphones work. During a recording, they watch meters that indicate sound levels and quality and adjust volume and tone controls accordingly. After recording sessions, technicians label and file tapes and discs for quick reference.

Although sound-recording technicians usually work in studios, sometimes they may be required to work in remote locations. For example, a symphony orchestra might choose to make a recording in a church because of its special organ. This means that the sound-recording technicians must transport their portable equipment to the church and set it up there. First, the technicians decide where to place the microphones for the best sound pickup. Then they usually monitor the recording from a sound truck outside. This truck often contains much of the same equipment that is found in a studio, including tape machines and sound quality meters.

Sound-recording technicians may have special titles depending on the type of machine they use. Some are called *disc-recording-machine operators* and some are *tape-recording-machine operators*. Those who record live television programs on magnetic tape are called *videotape-recording engineers*.

Education and training

As with all broadcast technician occupations, those who are interested should have a high school diploma. After high school, students should enroll in an approved community or technical college.

In high school, students should concentrate on mathematics and science courses. Students should also take any electronics courses offered, as well as classes in audio and video technology.

Sound-recording technicians who work in the radio and television industries must be licensed if their work involves operating transmitters.

Earnings

In the 1990s, students interested in this career will find employment opportunities to be very competitive, especially in large cities. Opportunities for entry-level positions may be better in small cities and towns. Technicians will be needed mainly to replace those workers who leave the field or who retire.

In general, sound-recording technicians at radio stations can expect to earn about $21,600 per year. Chief technicians can earn as much as $44,800. In television work, the average salary is about $20,000 per year.

Ways of getting more information

For more information about a career as a sound-recording technician, contact:

▶ Broadcast Education Association
1771 N Street, NW
Washington, DC 20036-2891

▶ At the location of the recording session, a sound-recording technician monitors the quality of the sound with his headphones.

▶ Federal Communications Commission
1919 M Street, NW
Washington, DC 20554

▶ National Association of Broadcast Employees and Technicians
7101 Wisconsin Avenue, Suite 800
Bethesda, MD 20814

Sound Technicians

Other articles to look at:
► **Audio-Control Technicians**
► **Cable-Television Technicians**
► **Electricians**
► **Recording Industry Workers**
► **Sound-Recording Technicians**

What sound technicians do

Sound technicians install, maintain, and repair sound systems that are used in businesses, offices, stores, and factories. These sound systems may be designed to play music, announce messages, or provide the sound portion of live or recorded lectures or entertainment.

Sound technicians usually work under the direction of a sound technician supervisor who has received instructions about what kinds of equipment and connections are required for a job. After receiving instructions from the supervisor, sound technicians put the sound equipment into position and secure it in place with brackets, clamps, or screws. They install and attach the wires and cables that connect the various parts of the system, such as speakers, amplifiers, microphones, and tape players. They also test the various parts of the system to see that they are functioning properly.

Not all sound systems work the same way. For example, the sound system in a dentist's office will play mostly soothing music at a low volume. The sound system in an airport or factory, on the other hand, is used to broadcast announcements and must be loud enough to be heard over the noise of engines, machines, and people's conversations. Sound technicians help their supervisors test the systems they install to be sure they work properly for their purpose and setting. They turn volume and control knobs to adjust sound levels to suit the size of the room, the level of other noises, and the uses to which the system is being put.

After the installation, sound technicians also repair and maintain the sound equipment as necessary.

Education and training

Sound technicians need to have at least a high school education. In addition, many employers prefer to hire applicants who have completed one or two years of post–high school training at a trade or vocational school or at a junior or community college.

While in high school, students interested in this kind of work should take courses in mathematics and science, especially courses that include instruction in electricity, electronics, and how sound travels. The mathematics courses should include algebra and geometry. Students should also take courses in English. They should be able to read safety rules, equipment and technical manuals, and other kinds of written instructions. They should be able to write reports with proper spelling, grammar, and punctuation.

▶ Sound systems are installed in most public shopping areas to add pleasant atmosphere.

Earnings

Sound systems will probably continue to be used in a wide variety of settings, and employment opportunities for sound technicians will probably remain fairly good in the 1990s.

The salaries of sound technicians vary according to the part of the country they work in and their level of education, experience, and responsibility. Most sound technicians are paid between $18,000 and $30,000 a year. A few, especially those with little experience or training, may make only around $14,000 a year, while some very experienced technicians may make as much as $36,000 a year or more.

Ways of getting more information

Working as an audiovisual aide or as a member of a stage crew will offer relevant experience.

In addition, students can write for more information from any of the following organizations:

▶ Electronic Industries Association
2001 Pennsylvania Avenue, NW, Suite 1100
Washington, DC 20006-1813

▶ International Society of Certified Electronics Technicians
2708 West Berry, Suite 3
Fort Worth, TX 76109

Speech-Language Pathologists

Other articles to look at:
- ▶ **Audiologists**
- ▶ **Health Therapists**
- ▶ **Psychologists**
- ▶ **Social Workers**

What speech-language pathologists do

Speech-language pathologists, or *speech therapists,* use prescribed tests to identify speech disorders in people and help them overcome their difficulties. The many speech disorders include difficulty making certain sounds, stuttering, or speaking quickly. Some people lose their ability to speak, either temporarily or totally. Most therapists work in schools, where they test students regularly for speech disorders. The students who have problems either receive therapy at the school or go to a speech clinic for treatment. There they receive physical therapy and help from psychologists and social workers. In some cases patients learn to develop entirely new speech skills, using tongue exercises and speech drills.

Speech therapy can be given individually or in groups. Usually, patients feel more comfortable when they work alone with a therapist. However, some people make more progress when they are placed with people who have similar speech problems. They seem to be encouraged by listening to the progress of others.

Not all speech therapists work in schools or privately owned speech clinics. Some work in hospitals, rehabilitation centers, and university speech clinics. Others conduct research into the causes and cures of speech disorders or teach in colleges and universities.

Education and training

Training to become a speech pathologist begins in college. Most states require that the pathologist have a master's degree in speech-language pathology before getting a job. More than 225 universities and colleges offer course work at this level.

Undergraduate courses usually include the study of the body (anatomy), child psychology, biology, physiology, and the study of speech and languages (linguistics, semantics, and phonetics).

High school teachers in public schools must earn a teacher's certificate and pass the state requirements for working with disabled children. Those who intend on practicing speech pathology outside of a school setting might need an additional 300 hours of work experience and also have to pass an examination.

Earnings

Opportunities for employment in the 1990s are expected to be very good in speech and hearing clinics, doctors' offices, nursing homes, rehabilitation centers, and home health agencies, where recovering stroke victims need therapy. There may also be a

▶ Pressing the student's hand to her throat, a speech therapist shows the student how the throat should move while speaking.

growing need for pathologists in elementary and high schools.

Speech-language pathologists' average yearly salary is about $23,400. The amount depends, however, on the individual's qualifications and experience. Those with many years' experience can earn up to $42,000 per year.

Ways of getting more information

For more information about a career as a speech pathologist, contact hospitals, rehabilitation centers, and therapy clinics. Ask to interview a speech therapist about his or her work. Volunteering to work in a clinic or hospital where you can become acquainted with

speech defects and their cures is a possibility, as is summer and part-time work in hospitals or clinics.

For more information about a career as a speech-language pathologist, write to the following agency:

▶ American Speech-Language-Hearing Association
10801 Rockville Pike
Rockville, MD 20852

Spies

Other articles to look at:
▶ **Detectives**
▶ **FBI Agents**
▶ **Foreign Service Officers**
▶ **Forensics Experts**
▶ **Private Investigators**

What spies do

Spies, also called *intelligence officers,* work for the U.S. government to gather secret information about the governments of foreign countries. This secret information, called intelligence, is one of the tools the U.S. government then uses to help make decisions about its own military, economic, and political policies.

There are two basic types of intelligence officers, *case officers,* also called *operators,* and *analysts.* Case officers are most often involved in the colorful and dangerous sorts of activities shown in the movies. They collect intelligence in the field, that is, they are typically stationed in foreign countries where they have frequent contact with other people who supply them with the valuable information they are seeking. Analysts, on the other hand, are more likely to be stationed in an office in Washington, D.C. (though some also work abroad), where they put many pieces of information together, interpreting and analyzing the data they have received from case officers and other sources. Analysts include *technical analysts,* who may gather data from satellites, and *cryptographic technicians,* who are experts at coding, decoding, and sending secret messages. Analysts make predictions and forecasts about what is likely to happen in a foreign country.

There are three categories of intelligence operations: strategic, tactical, and counterintelligence. People working in strategic intelligence keep track of world events, watch foreign leaders very carefully, and study a foreign country's politics, economy, and its people, as well as its military status and any scientific advances it may be making. Tactical intelligence-gathering involves collecting the same kind of information, but in combat areas and risky political settings abroad. Counterintelligence officers are assigned to protect U.S. secrets, institutions, and intelligence activities, and to identify and to prevent enemy operations that might hurt the United States, its citizens, or its allies. Such enemy plots would include world-wide terrorism and drug trafficking.

Intelligence officers work for the Central Intelligence Agency, the National Security Agency, and all branches of the U.S. military.

Education and training

All of the federal intelligence services are looking for people of high moral character, high academic credentials, and sincere patriotic commitment. A bachelor's degree is required, and an advanced degree preferred for some positions.

Candidates for field operations need to feel comfortable in social situations, make friends easily, and enjoy going out and doing things, some of which involve risk. They have to be able to think on their feet. Candidates for analyst positions typically have advanced degrees, are more studious, and are more comfortable working by themselves in an office. Both officers and analysts are trained on the job. Candidates who speak certain foreign languages, such as Russian or Chinese, have a big advantage.

Earnings

In the past, 50 percent of all U.S. intelligence activities were focused on the Soviet Union. The decline of communism in Eastern Europe and the former Soviet republics means that this major threat has been greatly reduced. However, the need for intelligence activities will remain high, as much attention will be turned to other unstable parts of the world.

Intelligence agencies are still concerned with many of the same issues, such as the spread of nuclear, chemical, and biological weapons, as well as some evolving issues, such as threats from foreign nuclear reactors and nuclear waste to the environment, natural resources, and worldwide human health.

The starting salary for intelligence officers with a bachelor's degree ranges from $20,000 to $29,000. Those with advanced degrees may start at $35,000; a candidate with an advanced degree in engineering or a physical science may start as high as $41,000. Experience, extra qualifications such as knowledge of a rare foreign language, and promotions bring higher salaries. Those in top management earn from $67,000 to $87,000 a year. Officers who work abroad receive free housing and special allowances and benefits.

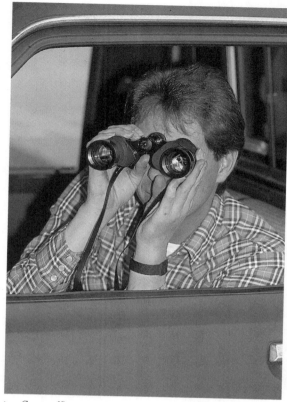

▶ Case officers gather much of their information while working undercover.

Ways of getting more information

Since intelligence agencies are by nature secretive, it is easiest to ask a school librarian about books on the subject.

For further information, write to:

▶ Association of Former Intelligence Officers
6723 Whittier Avenue, Suite 303A
McClean, VA 22101

Sporting Goods Production Workers

Other articles to look at:
▶ **Assemblers**
▶ **Molders**
▶ **Plastics Products Manufacturing Workers**
▶ **Quality-Control Technicians**
▶ **Toy Industry Workers**

What sporting goods production workers do

Team sports and personal physical fitness have come to enjoy widespread popularity in the 1990s. Professional and college sports teams dominate radio and television and the sports pages of newspapers. Health and racquet-sports clubs have become common sources of recreation for many people who live in the United States.

This sports and fitness boom has increased the demand for a wide variety of sports equipment, ranging from tennis and bowling balls to hockey and lacrosse sticks. As a result, workers are needed to produce this sports equipment. *Sporting goods production workers* operate the automated machinery that turns out sports equipment. In addition, many of these workers also hand-make equipment that cannot easily be produced by machines.

Many sporting goods production workers are *machine operators*. The machines they operate range from sewing machines to large, complex automated equipment. These machines heat, mold, stretch, cut, pound, and trim materials.

Assemblers are workers who put together the parts of products. These workers clean, paint, polish, stitch, weave, lace, glue, weld, or engrave objects. *Floor assemblers* work with power tools and large, automated machines. *Bench assemblers* do more exacting work, putting together small parts and testing finished products. *Precision assemblers* perform tasks that require special skills. These workers sometimes test new designs and products.

Many sporting goods productions workers are highly specialized. These workers include *hand baseball sewers, golf club assemblers, base fillers and stuffers, baseball glove shapers, inflated ball molders,* and *bowling ball engravers.*

There are some people who do custom work, meaning that they produce equipment, or even uniforms and costumes, one piece at a time, by hand and special smaller machines. For instance, a worker may produce custom-made ice skates for professional hockey players or Olympic-hopeful figure skaters. A specialized seamstress may sew only glittering costumes for professional ice dancers.

The quality of sporting goods is important, especially for equipment that is to be used in college and professional sports. Many team sports have strict rules and regulations regarding the size and shape of equipment as well as the materials used in manufacturing it. *Quality-control inspectors* make sure that all manufactured equipment conforms to these rules and regulations.

Education and training

For most manufacturing work, a high school diploma is desired, although it is not always necessary. New employees must often receive on-the-job training. Depending on the type of manufacturing operation involved, this training may last from just a few days up to several months.

People who work for themselves may learn how to produce hand-made sporting goods by first learning how to be, for example, an expert shoemaker or seamstress. They also might first become an apprentice at a small sporting goods manufacturer.

Earnings

Even though Americans are spending more of their time and money on recreation, much of the sports equipment is imported, causing a reduction in the need for manufacturing workers. There will be little change in the need for workers in this field during the 1990s.

Most sporting goods productions workers receive at least the minimum wage as a starting salary. Beginning pay ranges from $10,000 to $18,000 per year. Assemblers usually earn from $9,300 to $19,000 per year. Skilled machine operators earn a higher wage. Average pay for all sporting goods production workers is about $7.00 an hour.

Ways of getting more information

For more information about a career as a sporting goods production worker, contact the following agencies:

▶ A sporting goods production worker prepares footballs for the installment of the inflatable bladders.

▶ National Sporting Goods Association
   Lake Center Plaza Building
   1699 Wall Street
   Mt. Prospect, IL 60056-5780

▶ Sporting Goods Manufacturers' Association
   200 Castlewood Drive
   North Palm Beach, FL 33408

Sports Coaches

Other articles to look at:
▶ Aerobics Instructors
▶ Athletes
▶ Athletic Trainers
▶ Health Therapists
▶ Recreation Workers

What sports coaches do

There are organized sports teams at every age level and level of competition. For example, children as young as six and seven years of age can join baseball and soccer leagues. These same children can progress through pony leagues, little league sports, elementary school teams, and high school and college teams. As adults, some may even become members of professional sports teams or play on neighborhood or work-related teams.

All of these teams in all sports have one common element—a coach. *Sports coaches,* sometimes called *athletic coaches,* fall into two general categories: *head coaches* and *professional athlete coaches.* Head coaches lead teams of athletes. Professional athlete coaches often work with athletes in individual sports, and they are categorized by the sport they specialize in, such as tennis, swimming, or golf. In either case, the primary role of the coach is to teach and inspire players and to produce winners and winning teams.

Coaches must be very knowledgeable about the rules and strategies of their sport. They must be able to analyze the perform-ance of their players and to fit players into positions where they can contribute the most to their teams. Sports coaches observe their players while they perform in order to see whether they need improvement in any aspect of their playing. Often, the coaches themselves will demonstrate the sport to those they are coaching. For example, if a swimmer is just not getting his or her back-stroke right, the coach may jump in the water and show exactly how it should be done. This analysis often also involves videotaping play-ers and reviewing their performances. Whether they work with team sports or just one-on-one games, the coaches will watch the opponents to see what their strengths and weaknesses are so that this information can be used in their own players' strategy.

Coaches often work with *assistant coaches,* who usually concentrate on one specific as-pect of the sport. For example, baseball teams usually employ *pitching coaches, hitting coaches, outfield coaches,* and *first-* and *third-base coaches.* Football teams have *offensive coaches, defensive coaches, linebacker coaches,* and *quarterback coaches.* All of these assistant coaches work under the direction of the head coach.

Education and training

There are no specific educational require-ments for coaches. Many of today's coaches have college degrees because they played col-lege sports. Nevertheless, it is possible for anyone with knowledge and love of a sport and excellent leadership qualities to become a coach.

Coaches usually work their way up through the coaching system. Most begin as assistant coaches on little league or elementary school teams. These coaches may eventually become head coaches on high school or college teams. The very best of these coaches often go on to coach world-class athletes or professional sports teams.

Earnings

Americans are avid sports fans and enjoy both watching and playing team sports. Both young and old alike will participate in more sports during the 1990s, requiring more coaches to lead the players.

In the sports of professional football, basketball, and baseball, head coaches usually earn between $50,000 and $250,000 a year. A professional coach's salary is often directly related to how successful the coach has been in producing winning teams.

College coaches earn an average salary of about $35,000, although coaches at big universities often earn much more. High school coaches generally earn between $15,000 and $30,000 per year. In addition to coaching, high school coaches often teach classes as well.

Ways of getting more information

To obtain more information about a career as a sports coach, write to the following:

▶ American Alliance for Health, Physical Education, Recreation and Dance
  1900 Association Drive
  Reston, VA 22091

▶ A coach explains a plan of defense for the game to his basketball team.

▶ Athletic Institute
  200 Castlewood Drive
  North Palm Beach, FL 33408

▶ Society of State Directors of Health, Physical Education and Recreation
  9805 Hillridge Drive
  Kensington, MD 20895

Stage Production Workers

Other articles to look at:
▶ **Designers**
▶ **Directors, Movies and Television**
▶ **Light Technicians**
▶ **Sound Technicians**
▶ **Stage Technicians**

What stage production workers do

Stage production workers work behind the scenes of plays or other theatrical performances, handling a variety of tasks to add to the impact of the performance and keep it running smoothly. Because they are involved with all aspects of the performance, their specific responsibilities vary according to their job title. Stage production work is necessary for plays, operas, ballets, and other performances in theaters. These workers can also find work with concerts, lectures, and award ceremonies and dinners.

Concert managers or *lecture hall managers* supervise the theater itself. They manage the ticket takers and ushers, maintain the physical building, order food for the refreshment counter and other supplies, and are on hand during performances to answer questions and handle problems. *Road production general managers* perform basically the same tasks when a play goes on tour (meaning that the production travels to other cities). They also arrange for housing for the crew and cast, handle advertising and promotion, and oversee the hiring of any stagehands while on tour.

Stage directors are in charge of the actual production of the play itself. They hire the cast and supervise rehearsals, and go on to work with playwrights, producers, set and costume designers, lighting and sound technicians, and stage managers to make sure the play is presented as effectively as possible.

There are all kinds of other backstage workers. *Set designers* design and supervise the construction of the scenery, and *costume designers* design and supervise the buying or making of the costumes; each of them has assistants and crews working under them. *Prop managers* are in charge of finding, buying, or making all the things the actors and actresses use on stage. The technical designers and workers are the people who plan and operate the lighting and sound effects needed to make the play truly dramatic. Finally, there is the *stage manager,* who acts as a sort of director's assistant to coordinate all the various parts of backstage work.

Education and training

Although there are no specific educational requirements for stage production workers, a high school diploma is usually required, and a college degree is highly recommended. Drama courses and experience in school theatrical performances are obvious pluses, and other specific skills are also helpful, such as design or fine arts for set and costume designers and business courses for concert hall and road production managers. Courses in drawing, painting, sewing, woodwork, architectural drawing, and shop are all helpful preparations for a career in stage production.

Most stage production workers begin by volunteering their services or by working part-time in a position not directly related to the one they really want. Set designers might start as members of the set construction crew; a director might begin as an assistant stage manager. Gradually the skilled worker may work his or her way up to the desired position. It should be noted that the competition for theatrical work is very keen, and even experienced workers often work part-time or in assistant positions.

Earnings

Salaries for stage production workers vary enormously, depending on the experience of the worker, specific job responsibilities, location of the theater, and budget of the performance. Successful Broadway directors may earn well over $200,000 a year; struggling regional or off-Broadway directors may have to supplement their income by waiting tables. Some jobs are governed by union rates, which means the hourly, daily, or weekly rate may be quite good. Keep in mind that few stage production workers work year-round; many of them only work part-time and must have other jobs.

Ways of getting more information

Getting involved with school or community theatrical performances is the best way to test interests and talents in this field.

For more information about stage production work, write to:

▶ A stage production worker hems a costume for a cast member.

▶ International Alliance of Theatrical Stage Employees and Moving Picture Machine Operators of the U.S. and Canada
   1515 Broadway, Suite 601
   New York, NY 10036

▶ Society of Stage Directors and Choreographers
   1501 Broadway, 31st floor
   New York, NY 10036

Stage Technicians

Other articles to look at:
- ▶ **Audiovisual Technicians**
- ▶ **Carpenters**
- ▶ **Electricians**
- ▶ **Light Technicians**
- ▶ **Stage Production Workers**

What stage technicians do

Stage technicians install lights, sound equipment, and scenery for theater stages. They also build the stages for theatrical and musical events in parks, stadiums, and other places.

In carrying out a project, stage technicians use diagrams of the stage and written instructions from the stage designer. They confer with the stage manager to decide what kinds of sets, scenery, props, lighting, and sound equipment are required.

Then they collect or build the props or scenery, using hammers, saws, and other hand and power tools. Often they must climb ladders, scaffolding, or beams near the ceiling to connect cables or ropes that are used to raise and lower curtains or scenery.

Stage technicians also position lights and sound equipment on or around the stage. They clamp light fixtures to supports and connect electrical wiring from the fixtures to power sources and control panels.

The sound equipment used on and around stages usually includes microphones, speakers, and amplifiers. Technicians position this equipment and attach the wires that connect it to power sources and to the sound-mixing equipment that controls the volume and quality of the sound.

During rehearsals and performances, stage technicians may pull ropes and cables that raise and lower curtains and other equipment. Sometimes they also operate the lighting and sound equipment.

Education and training

Stage technicians usually must be high school graduates. In addition, many employers prefer to hire stage technicians who are graduates of two-year junior or community colleges. While in high school, people interested in this career should take college-preparatory courses, including algebra and geometry and English courses that develop their reading and writing skills.

During their post–high school training, students should take any available courses in theater arts or related subjects, along with general-studies courses, especially in English and music. They should also take carpentry or electronics, especially courses that include work with lighting and sound.

Earnings

It is almost impossible to foresee what employment opportunities for stage technicians will be like in the future. The demand for stage technicians is determined by the amount of live entertainment that is being offered, and that is strongly influenced by over-

▶ A stage technician checks the positions of spotlights during a technical rehearsal.

all economic conditions. If the economy remains strong, employment opportunities should be good.

Most stage technicians earn between $20,000 and $30,000 a year; however, salaries vary widely depending on the employer, geographic location, and the technician's level of responsibility.

Stage technicians who are hired mostly for their skills as carpenters, electricians, or sound or light technicians earn salaries roughly equal to the salaries received by those workers. The salaries for most workers in these careers range from $14,000 to $30,000 a year, with carpenters generally at the low end and electricians at the high end.

Ways of getting more information

Probably the best way to learn more about this kind of work is through personal experience as a stage hand helping to put on a school show or play. Another way of getting more information is to arrange a visit to a local theater where students can meet and talk to stage technicians.

In addition, students can write to the following organization for more information:

▶ Theatre Communications Group
355 Lexington Avenue
New York, NY 10017

State Police Officers

Other articles to look at:
- ▶ **FBI Agents**
- ▶ **Fire Fighters**
- ▶ **Forensic Experts**
- ▶ **Lawyers**
- ▶ **Police Officers**

What state police officers do

If a car is going 20 miles an hour over the speed limit and a city or town police officer from a local force chases the driver onto an interstate highway, the two cars could easily leave the borders of one town or county and go into another, where the police officer would have no jurisdiction and would therefore be unable to write a ticket or make an arrest. However, if a *state police officer* made the chase, he or she would be able to make an arrest because state officers can enforce the law anywhere within the borders of their state. State police officers patrol our highways and enforce highway safety laws. The state police is a fairly new agency, started within the last 100 years. Highway use is one example of why the state police came into being.

As highway safety officers, state police ride in patrol cars looking out for dangerous situations. They write traffic tickets, give warnings, and watch for stolen vehicles. They also help drivers who are having trouble with their cars or trucks. If there is a highway accident, state police officers take charge at the scene, directing traffic, calling for emergency equipment, and giving first aid.

In addition to highway safety, state police officers do some general police work such as keeping order and catching criminals. *Detectives* and *investigators* work in plainclothes and try to gather information about criminals. They look over the scene of a crime, collect evidence, question witnesses, and write reports. After a criminal has been caught, detectives appear in court and give the evidence they have collected.

Education and training

Each state has its own special requirements for its officers, but some apply to all states. Candidates for state police jobs must be U.S. citizens and pass a tough examination. They must also have a high school diploma, be at least twenty-one, and have a valid driver's license. The best-prepared candidates will have taken some college courses in subjects such as English, government, and criminal justice. Police training with one of the armed forces is also very helpful. In addition, candidates have to pass difficult physical tests because officers must have better than average strength and stamina.

Once candidates are accepted into a training program, they take classes in such areas as their state's laws, self-defense, first aid, and how to handle firearms.

Experienced officers are usually able to advance by taking college classes in police science and law enforcement. Officers move up on the basis of job performance, outside training, and good conduct. The usual way to move up the ranks is from private, to corporal, to sergeant, to first sergeant, to lieutenant, and finally to captain.

Earnings

It is expected that state patrols will need more officers in the 1990s. Competition for these jobs will be heavy as more and more people try to enter this field. Many people are attracted to this field because of good salaries and benefits. Those with a college education in law enforcement should have the best opportunities.

State police officers can earn an average yearly salary of about $26,700. Earnings vary by region and size of the department.

Police officers usually receive special allowances for such items as uniforms, revolvers, nightsticks, handcuffs, and other necessary equipment. Paid vacation and medical insurance are common as extra benefits. Also, because of good pension plans, many officers retire and receive half-pay after about 25 years of service.

Ways of getting more information

The best way to prepare for the job is to take classes in English and government and to learn to be a good driver through driver's education classes.

Write to the following for more information on state police officers:

▶ A state police officer lectures a class on drug related problems.

▶ American Police Academy
Lock Box 15350
Chevy Chase, MD 20815

Stenographers

Other articles to look at:
- ▶ **Bookkeepers**
- ▶ **Court Reporters**
- ▶ **Medical Record Administrators**
- ▶ **Receptionists**
- ▶ **Secretaries**

What stenographers do

Stenographers write down what people say as they say it. This is called taking dictation. Because they have to work very quickly, stenographers use shorthand, a set of symbols that stand for words and parts of words. They may write shorthand or use a stenotype machine that types shorthand symbols. Then they transcribe their shorthand notes and type them up into letters, reports, or other documents. Stenographers are also called *stenotype operators.*

Using a stenographer saves time; instead of writing out letters and memos, the stenographers' employers can simply tell the stenographer what they want to say. The stenographer returns a finished document.

General stenographers take routine dictation and do other office tasks such as typing, filing, and answering telephones. Experienced stenographers take more difficult dictations; for example, they may sit in on staff meetings and later give word-for-word records or summary reports of the meetings. Experienced stenographers may also supervise other stenographers and office clerical workers.

Some stenographers develop special skills. Technical stenographers master the terms of a specialized field such as law, medicine, or engineering. Some stenographers can take dictation in foreign languages.

Other stenographers, called *shorthand reporters,* are responsible for making the official records of government meetings. Shorthand reporters may record a meeting of the U.S. Congress or a state legislature or other government agency. Accuracy is extremely important. Many shorthand reporters use a computer system, called Computer-Aided Transcription, which can translate shorthand notes into English.

Education and training

Stenographers need a high school diploma. High school courses in typing, shorthand, and business English are absolutely necessary. Business schools and vocational schools also teach stenographic skills. Getting jobs and advancement will depend on a stenographer's speed and accuracy at both taking dictation and typing. The federal government requires stenographers to take dictation at 80 words a minute and type 40 words a minute. Many shorthand reporters must be able to take dictation at 225 words a minute.

Earnings

There will be a declining number of job openings for stenographers in the 1990s because so many offices now use dictation machines.

▶ A stenographer takes dictation from her employer, using a shorthand method of writing that saves time.

However, the federal government as well as state and local governments and conferences will continue to need skilled shorthand reporters.

Stenographers working in private industry earn about $21,500 per year. Shorthand reporters generally earn a little bit more. Earnings, however, depend on speed, education, and experience.

Ways of getting more information

Acting as a club or organization's secretary would be a good introduction to work as a stenographer.

For more information, write to:

▶ Association of Independent Colleges and Schools
1 Dupont Circle, NW, Suite 350
Washington, DC 20036

▶ National Shorthand Reporters Association
118 Park Street, SE
Vienna, VA 22180

Stevedores

Other articles to look at:
▶ **Border Patrol Officers**
▶ **Industrial-Truck Operators**
▶ **Merchant Marines**
▶ **Military Careers**
▶ **Operating Engineers**

What stevedores do

When a ship comes into a busy port, *stevedores* are there ready to unload the cargo and deliver it to trucks. When the ship's cargo hold is empty, stevedores reload it and make sure all is in order before the ship leaves the pier and heads for another port. A ship's cargo usually consists of very large items, like cars, crates, and steel beams. The cargo is loaded or unloaded using huge mechanized magnets or hooks.

Stevedores, also called *longshore workers,* first dock ships by tying lines. Their work then breaks down into several categories: *dock workers* handle cargo on the pier, while *hold workers* go into the ship's hold (that is, they go onto the ship where the cargo is located), remove cargo from hooks, and stow it in place. *Winch operators* handle the winches, which are machines that control the booms that raise or lower cargo from the ship's deck. *Drivers* operate the forklift trucks, cranes, and other equipment. *Gear workers* maintain and repair the nets that prevent cargo that is accidentally dropped from the boom from falling into the water.

Sometimes, stevedores must operate machines that spurt such items as grain into the ship's cargo area. A worker would move the machine's controls to start and stop the flow of grain from spouts positioned over hatches aboard the ship. Stevedores also work with liquid cargo, such as vegetable oils, molasses, and chemicals.

The title *stevedores,* besides referring to the field in general, is also the name of one job in particular. The stevedore is in charge of stowing the cargo on a vessel as well as being in charge of all the workers on board. On large ships there can be as many as 250 longshore workers loading and unloading cargo.

Finally, *pier superintendents* are in charge of the operations of the entire pier. They study the layout of the ship so they know where the cargo should go—for example, cargo that is to be delivered at the next port must be loaded last. They know how many workers they need for the number of ships arriving, and they then hire those workers. They figure out how much the operation of their pier costs, and they make sure the bills are both sent out and collected.

Education and training

Stevedores must be physically strong and have plenty of stamina. Sometimes, they must work 24 hours at a time because ships need to go in and out of ports so quickly. Their work is very demanding and can sometimes be dangerous. Because of this, workers must be constantly alert and able to follow instructions.

Those who are in supervisor's jobs must have a good understanding of the entire operation of loading and unloading a ship. These workers often receive their training from one of the several U.S. maritime academies.

Earnings

In the 1990s, although work is usually not guaranteed, there may continue to be a demand for stevedores in some areas of the country. The Great Lakes area, for example, is in need of trained workers. It has only been fairly recently that ocean-going ships could sail these inland lakes, and so the stevedoring industry there is not well developed. In other areas, automated loaders have taken the places of some stevedores, but there is still a need for full-time trained longshore workers.

Stevedores' earnings average about $15.00 to $17.00 per hour. Longshore workers on the East Coast who worked full-time year-round earned a base salary of $25,000 in the early 1990s. Pier superintendents made between $20,000 and $35,000 per year, depending on the area of the country.

▶ Stevedores guide lift operators to move cables into place to unload freight from a ship.

Ways of getting more information

For more information about stevedoring careers write to the following:

▶ The International Longshoremen's and Warehousemen's Union
   1188 Franklin Street
   San Francisco, CA 94109

▶ International Longshoremen's Association
   17 Battery Place, Room 1530
   New York, NY 10004

Stockbrokers

What stockbrokers do

Stockbrokers represent both individuals and organizations in the buying and selling of what is called stock. When people buy stock, or shares, in a company, they actually own part of the company. Company managers use the money from the sale of stock to try to make the company more profitable. When the price of a stock goes up, stock owners may decide to sell their shares to make a profit. If they sell when the price has gone down, they have to take a loss. The price at any given time depends on the demand for the stock.

Stockbrokers may also be called *securities sales workers* or *account executives*. They perform a variety of duties. They open accounts for new customers. In doing so, they have to gather certain information from customers, which is required before customers can buy and sell stocks through a stockbroker's company. To buy and sell the stock, brokers send the information to the floor of a stock exchange, which is a place where stocks are bought and sold.

Stockbrokers give information to customers about the future outlook of companies.

They may give advice to customers about when to buy or sell certain stocks. They must be prepared to answer any question customers may have about how the stock market operates. They have to keep accurate records of all stock sales and purchases made on behalf of customers. In addition, they have to find new customers.

Stockbrokers are employed by companies known as brokerage houses, which are located throughout the country. During busy times, brokers may have to work overtime to keep up with paperwork. They may work fewer hours when they have few customer orders to carry out.

Education and training

Most brokerage houses will hire only people with college degrees. Some prefer those with degrees in business management and finance. Employees are given on-the-job training at most brokerage houses.

Almost all states require stockbrokers to be licensed. They are sometimes given written tests. Stockbrokers also have to register as representatives of their company. In doing so, they must obey the rules of the stock exchange they deal with or the rules of the National Association of Securities Dealers. To become a registered representative, stockbrokers must also pass a test.

Earnings

The job outlook for stockbrokers is usually good during periods when the nation's econ-

▶ A stockbroker calls up the current prices for a stock on his computer terminal.

omy is thriving. As more companies are formed and need to grow, more stock will need to be sold. Also, opportunities are good when individuals have more money to invest in the stock market. In other words, demand for stockbrokers goes up and down with the economy. Many beginning brokers are unable to find and keep enough customers, so they leave the field. This creates more job openings. Competition in this field is usually very tough.

The average salary of beginners is about $28,000 per year. Larger companies pay a somewhat higher starting wage. Once stockbrokers have enough customers, they work only on a commission basis. Experienced stockbrokers dealing with individual investors ca average about $71,000 per year. Those who helped institutions invest money can earn as much as $240,000 per year. In addition, brokerage houses may pay annual bonuses to brokers.

Ways of getting more information

Visiting a brokerage or a stock exchange in or near your community is an excellent introduction to this career.

For more information write to:

▶ American Stock Exchange
86 Trinity Place
New York, NY 10006

▶ New York Stock Exchange
11 Wall Street
New York, NY 10005

▶ Securities Industry Association
120 Broadway
New York, NY 10271

Structural-Steel Workers

Other articles to look at:
- ▶ **Construction Workers**
- ▶ **Forge Shop Workers**
- ▶ **Iron and Steel Industry Workers**
- ▶ **Operating Engineers**
- ▶ **Welders**

What structural-steel workers do

Structural-steel workers put up and put together the metal beams, columns, and frames that form what is called the skeleton of a building. Also called *ironworkers,* they work together as a team to raise up these heavy metal parts, place them in position, and join them together. Welding, riveting, and bolting are the usual ways of joining metal, and structural-steel workers must be good at all three. Besides large buildings, these skilled workers help build bridges and metal storage tanks.

There are several specialties within the structural-steel trade. Some structural-steel employees work as riggers and machine movers. They set up the equipment that hoists steel beams to be positioned by other workers. After deciding the best way for the steel part to be moved, they attach it to the proper lifting machines. *Reinforcing metalworkers* position the steel rods or steel mesh around which concrete is poured for columns, arches, domes, walls, and floors. *Ornamental iron-workers* put together metal stairways, doors, and cabinets. They build safes for banks and install iron fences, gates, and lampposts.

Structural-steel workers usually work outdoors and in very high places. Workers must be strong and steady, have a good sense of balance, and not be afraid of heights. They may have periods of unemployment between jobs and during bad or cold weather.

Education and training

The usual way of becoming a structural-steel worker is to complete an apprenticeship program. The International Association of Bridge, Structural and Ornamental Iron Workers can provide information on getting into these programs. An apprenticeship lasts three years and combines on-the-job training and classroom instruction. Apprentices learn to do ornamental iron and steel work, steel reinforcing, structural-steel work, and welding. Each year the apprentice also takes at least 144 hours of classes in welding, blueprint reading, use of tools, and other construction-industry skills.

Earnings

Although machines are replacing many human workers in the construction industry, there will continue to be demand for structural-steel workers. There is expected to be a rising need for certain buildings and highway and bridge construction, as well as for maintenance work on structures that are already built.

Salaries for structural-steel workers are often discussed in terms of earnings per week.

▶ A structural steel worker guides support beams into place during building construction.

Average weekly earnings for these workers is about $506. Ornamental ironworkers earn about the same amount of wages as structural workers. Workers usually receive twice their hourly rate for overtime hours. The starting pay for apprentices is about 40 to 60 percent of the salary that skilled workers receive.

Ways of getting more information

By taking a field trip to a construction site, young people can watch structural-steel workers in action and see how their work coordinates with that of other construction workers.

For more information about structural-steel workers and their jobs write to the following:

▶ Associated General Contractors of America
  1957 E Street, NW
  Washington, DC 20006

▶ International Association of Bridge, Structural and Ornamental Iron Workers
  1750 New York Avenue, NW
  Washington, DC 20006

Studio Technicians

Other articles to look at:
- ▶ **Audio-Control Technicians**
- ▶ **Drafters**
- ▶ **Electronics Technicians**
- ▶ **Recording Industry Workers**
- ▶ **Sound-Recording Technicians**

What studio technicians do

Studio technicians, or *sound mixers,* are concerned with the quality of audio recordings made during the production of radio and television programs and the sound recordings made during the production of records, tapes, and compact discs. They set up and monitor sound recording equipment and operate consoles (control panels with dials and switches) to regulate the sound volume as it is being recorded.

Studio technicians control a variety of factors that influence the quality of sound recordings. They set up different combinations and arrangements of microphones and amplifiers in the studio to best achieve the desired sound for the production. In addition to arranging the equipment, they turn the microphones on and off so that they are only working when needed. This keeps unwanted sounds from being recorded. Technicians also let actors, actresses, and other performers know which microphones are on and how loud or soft their voices (or instruments) should be.

Studio technicians work closely with *audio-control technicians, sound-recording techni-* *cians,* and other members of the broadcast production team. Before a program begins, these technicians may meet and discuss the needs of a particular production. During the taping of a program, the studio technician will often communicate with other crew members through a headset. Although the studio technician works under the supervision of the director of a production, the director often relies on the expertise of the sound technician to improve the quality of a recording.

Technicians not only set up and operate the sound recording equipment, they also maintain the equipment so that it is in good working condition. They use testing equipment such as a voltage meter to make sure the electrical wires are connected and there are no other defects. Technicians will often repair or replace broken sound recording equipment.

Education and training

Studio technicians need the electronics training and hand coordination necessary to operate technical equipment. They also should have good communication skills and be able to work closely with other audio-production workers.

The best way to become a studio technician is to have a high school degree and at least some electronics training. Many community colleges and technical schools have programs in electronics that provide the background necessary for success in this field. Knowledge of computers is also helpful, as computers are becoming more and more important in radio and TV broadcasting.

All studio technicians are given on-the-job training and spend the first several months working under the supervision of experienced technicians. New workers are closely supervised as they set up microphones and do other necessary tasks.

Earnings

Although there are many radio and television stations and sound recording studios in operation, the number of available technician jobs may decrease because of the increased use of computers. Also, partly because many people find it exciting to working as part of a production crew, there will be stiff competition for these positions. Those without much experience may have more success in smaller cities, where there are not as many job seekers.

The average salary at radio stations is about $21,600 per year, with those working for television stations earning somewhat more than other technicians. Those employed in large cities will earn about twice as much as those in smaller communities. This is a major reason why there is less competition for jobs in smaller communities.

Ways of getting more information

High school radio and television courses are a good way to gain some experience actually working on a production.

In addition, write to the following organizations and ask for information about being a studio technician:

▶ The sound board and recording tapes are continually monitored by the studio technician.

▶ Broadcast Education Association
  1771 N Street, NW
  Washington, DC 20036-2891

▶ National Association of Broadcast Employees and Technicians
  7101 Wisconsin Avenue, Suite 800
  Bethesda, MD 20814

Stunt Persons

Other articles to look at:
▶ **Actors and Actresses**
▶ **Athletes**

What stunt persons do

The action in movies and television gets wilder every year. People jump out of helicopters, run through burning or exploding buildings, crash cars, and get knocked off horses and motorcycles. While all these dangers appear genuine on the screen, they are really illusions, the work of movie technicians and stunt persons.

Stunt persons are actors and actresses who specialize in performing dangerous scenes. For their performances, they train more like athletes than actors. They usually don't talk on the screen, but they place themselves in scenarios where someone could get seriously hurt. Often movie and television stars who are supposed to do physically dangerous things have stunt persons stand in for them.

While they specialize in dangerous stunts, stunt persons have to take great care that they are not hurt while filming. Air bags, body padding, and cables are often used to protect the stunt person taking a huge fall or being thrown from a motorcycle. Special fire-proof clothing and skin creams protect them in scenes involving fire. For unique stunts, the stunt person may design and build special protective equipment. The risks that a stunt person takes are always calculated risks.

The idea for a stunt is born inside a writer's head and is written into the script. The director of the movie or TV show then must determine how it will appear on screen. Through a loose network of stunt experts in the industry, the director will find someone who can do a certain type of stunt (such as diving off bridges into rivers) particularly well. For large action-packed movies, this work is usually done by the stunt coordinator, who organizes all the stunt activities and hires the stunt persons.

Next, the stunt person and the stunt coordinator work with the director on how to execute the stunt. The first concern is the safety of the stunt person. A professional stunt person always knows when something is too risky, and must work to make the risk more acceptable. The director then works out the camera angles that will give the stunt its maximum impact and hide the safety equipment being used.

Next, the scene is set up. This can take a very long time, because dozens of movie technicians have to coordinate their work. A scene that takes only a few seconds on screen can take five or six hours to set up. When everything is in place, the stunt person goes through with the stunt. Often the stunt will have to be filmed a number of times.

Stunt persons can sometimes move up to become stunt coordinators for films. Those with some acting ability may be able to get speaking parts or even starring roles in films. Other stunt persons find work in water ski shows and thrill-seeker shows that travel the country.

Education and Training

No standard training exists for stunt persons. They usually start out by contacting stunt coordinators and asking for work. If the stunt coordinator thinks the person has the proper credentials, he or she will be hired for basic stunt work like fight scenes.

Much of the learning takes place on the job. Every new type of stunt has its own particular problems that must be solved. By working closely with the expert stunt coordinators in the movie industry, stunt people can learn how to eliminate most of the risks involved in stunts.

Stunt persons must work out to stay in top shape. They often learn stage fighting, which looks realistic but doesn't hurt anyone. They also need to learn how to take a fall in such a way that they don't hurt themselves. Nevertheless, injuries are very common among stunt persons, and the possibility of death is always present in more dangerous stunts.

Earnings

Stunt persons are paid the same day rate as other actors, plus an extra dividend for the complexity of the stunt. More dangerous stunts generally pay a higher dividend. Stunt persons must belong to the actor's union, the Screen Actor's Guild. The SAG minimum day rate is $448.

Stunt persons are only paid for the days they work, so injuries can hurt a stunt person's income as well. Stunt coordinators are hired for a longer period of time to work on a particular movie, and are paid much more.

▶ Being thrown from an exploding car is all part of a day's work for a stunt person.

Ways of getting more information

To learn more about becoming a stunt person, write to:

▶ Screen Actor's Guild
7065 Hollywood Boulevard
Hollywood, CA 90028

Surgeons

Other articles to look at:
▶ **Health Therapists**
▶ **Hospital Attendants**
▶ **Medical Technicians**
▶ **Nurse Practitioners**
▶ **Physicians**

What surgeons do

Surgeons are physicians who specialize in performing operations. They operate on patients to repair injuries; to remove diseased parts of the body; and to fix deformed parts of the body.

Some surgeons, called *general surgeons,* perform many different kinds of operations. Other surgeons specialize in certain operations or parts of the body. For example, some surgeons operate on the brain and spinal cord. Others work on fixing broken bones. Some specialize in heart bypasses and heart transplants.

Surgeons first examine their patients, learn about their medical histories, and study the results of any physical tests. They work with a patient's physician and other medical professionals to decide if the patient needs surgery. Surgeons explain the operation to the patient; they decide what kind of surgery will work the best.

During the operation, the surgeon is the head of the medical team that works on the patient. The team will include an *anesthesiologist* (this person will give the patient certain medication so that the patient will not feel any pain, or they will have the patient breathe a certain gas to put them to sleep during the operation), surgical assistants, and nurses. Medical students may watch the operation to learn how to do it. After operations, surgeons continue to check on their patients and see that they are on their way to recovery.

Surgeons use many kinds of instruments during operations. For example, a surgeon may cut out diseased tissue with sharp cutting tools or with lasers. During their careers, surgeons must keep studying new methods and learning how to use new technology.

Surgeons work in hospitals and clinics. They often work under pressure because operations can be a matter of life or death for their patients. They also work long hours. They may have to perform emergency operations at night, on weekends, or on their days off. Difficult operations may involve hours of standing and demand great concentration, skill, and steadiness.

Education and training

Becoming a surgeon takes many years of hard work—up to 14 years of study and training. In high school, students should get a well-rounded education. Biology or chemistry are good majors for students planning on becoming surgeons. While they are in college, students take the Medical College Admission Test. Medical schools use these test scores to decide which students to accept.

After graduating from college, students spend four years in medical school. For two of these years they will concentrate on classroom and laboratory work; during the last two years, students start working with patients in hospitals.

After completing medical school, surgeons spend three to six years in a hospital residency program. As residents, they can perform operations under the supervision of the hospital's surgeons.

At the end of their training, surgeons must be certified before they can practice. To earn certification, they have to pass an examination that is administered by the state in which they wish to practice.

Earnings

Because there are more and more elderly people in the population and more and more new surgical techniques being introduced, the need for surgeons is expected to grow in the 1990s. The need to replace surgeons who leave the profession is low because most surgeons stay in their careers until they retire.

Surgeons earn some of the highest salaries of all occupations. Average yearly income is about $132,300. Some specialists earn even more. However, the education and training period for physicians and especially surgeons is long. Surgeons just out of medical school can expect to earn about $24,000 to $31,000 per year. Once they are established, their incomes rise rapidly.

Ways of getting more information

You may be able to interview a surgeon or a physician about how they go about performing surgery. A librarian can help you find books and articles about surgeons and surgery.

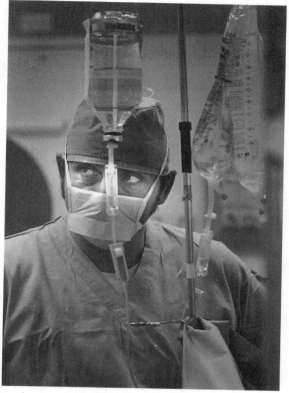

▶ A surgeon checks the patient's heart monitor during an operation.

For more information, write to the following agencies:

▶ American Medical Association
515 North State Street
Chicago, IL 60610

▶ Association of American Medical Colleges
1 Dupont Circle, NW
Washington, DC 20036

Surveying and Mapping Technicians

Other articles to look at:
► **Archaeologists**
► **Cartographers**
► **Civil Engineers**
► **Drafters**
► **Surveyors**

What surveying and mapping technicians do

The Egyptians employed surveyors to determine land holdings. The Romans used surveyors to map the principal roads of the Roman Empire. Today, surveyors help to establish property boundaries, lay out new communities, and establish the precise locations of new roads, bridges, dams, and other structures. *Surveying and mapping technicians* help civil engineers, mapmakers, and professional surveyors determine, describe, and record geographic areas and features.

Surveying and mapping technicians work in a survey party, under the supervision of engineering professionals. These technicians are often responsible for setting up, adjusting, and taking readings from delicate surveying instruments. Some technicians adjust and operate instruments called theodolites, which measure vertical and horizontal angles of land or buildings. Technicians or their helpers must hold certain rods in place so that the theodolite can be focused on the correct site, somewhat like an object that is viewed through a camera lens. Some technicians

work with equipment that electronically measures distances, or they may have to hand-hold measuring tape and chains if such electronic equipment is not used. As these readings are taken, the technicians must keep careful field notes so that surveying reports will be accurate. Often they must enter the information from the readings into computers.

For land surveying, technicians must be skilled in measuring property boundaries, reading maps, and interpreting land deeds. Preparing legal documents, such as deeds and leases, is also part of the technicians' work.

Technicians may also do highway, pipeline, railway, or powerline surveying. *Geodetic surveying technicians* take measurements of large masses of land, sea, and space.

Technicians who work for hydrographic surveying firms make surveys of harbors, rivers, and other bodies of water. These surveys help engineers to plan breakwaters, dams, locks, piers, and bridges.

Mining companies also use surveying and mapping technicians. These technicians use instruments that establish the boundaries of mining claims and also show features of the earth that indicate the presence of such valuable natural resources as certain ores.

Topographical surveying is another area where surveying technicians are employed. Topographical surveys establish the contours of the land. They show such features as mountains, lakes, forests, farms, and other landmarks. Technicians who do this type of surveying often take serial and land photographs with special cameras that photograph large areas of land. Such photographs allow accurate measurements to be made of land where roads, railway lines, and other engineering projects are planned.

Education and training

Surveying and mapping is highly technical work. A high school diploma is required. Students should take college-preparatory classes that include all of the mathematics, science, and communications courses available. Courses in mechanical drawing and drafting are also helpful.

After high school, students should enroll in a junior college or technical school that offers training in surveying and mapping. These programs usually last two years and often include summer field study. Surveying firms often provide additional on-the-job training.

Earnings

In the 1990s, job opportunities for surveying and mapping technicians should be good if the expected growth in construction occurs.

The average yearly salary for full-time technicians is about $21,800. However, some earn as much as $41,000 per year.

Ways of getting more information

For more information, write:

▶ Accreditation Board for Engineering and Technology
345 East 47th Street
New York, NY 10017

▶ A surveying technician holds up a measuring pole so that the surveyor at the other end can take distance and height measurements.

▶ American Congress on Surveying and Mapping
5410 Grosvenor Lane, Suite 100
Bethesda, MD 20814

Surveyors

Other articles to look at:
- ▶ **Cartographers**
- ▶ **Civil Engineering Technicians**
- ▶ **Civil Engineers**
- ▶ **Geographers**
- ▶ **Surveying and Mapping Technicians**

What surveyors do

Surveyors use a variety of mechanical and electronic devices to measure exact distances and locate positions on the earth's surface. These geographic measurements are used in many ways: to determine property boundaries, for mapmaking, and in construction and engineering projects. Wherever it is necessary to establish exact locations and measure points, surveyors make an accurate and detailed survey of the area.

Exactly what surveyors do depends on their area of expertise and the type of job they are working on. Some work on proposed construction projects such as highways, airstrips, housing developments, and bridges to provide the necessary measurements before the engineers and construction crews begin work. Some help mapmakers chart unexplored regions; others survey land claims, bodies of water, and underground mines; still others clear the right-of-way for water pipes, drainage ditches, or telephone lines. Some measure areas of land, sea, or space that are so large that the measurements must take into account the curvature of the earth; others use special photographic equipment installed in airplanes or ground stations to chart areas that are hard to reach in person.

Whatever their area of specialization, surveyors must enjoy working outdoors in all sorts of weather, must be comfortable with the mathematics necessary to make exact measurements, must have the aptitude to work with a variety of mechanical and electronic measuring devices, and must possess the leadership qualities to direct and supervise the work of people on their surveying team.

Education and training

While a person can become a surveyor's helper with just a high school diploma, the more technical and professional jobs require at least some college education. Junior colleges and technical schools offer courses, ranging from one to three years, that prepare students for positions as surveying technicians. Those who wish to become surveyors will need a bachelor's degree in surveying, civil engineering, or one of the physical sciences from an approved four-year college. And to advance in some of the more technical specialties, graduate study beyond a bachelor's degree is recommended.

All 50 states require that land surveyors making property and boundary surveys be licensed or registered. The requirements vary from state to state but in general include a college degree, several years of experience,

▶ A surveyor checks the distance of an object.

and the ability to pass a surveying examination. More and more, the trend is to require at least a bachelor's degree in engineering to be registered as a professional surveyor.

Earnings

The employment outlook in surveying through the 1990s is expected to be fairly good. As the field becomes more technically sophisticated, however, applicants who have degrees will win the best positions.

The average salary for registered land surveyors working for the federal government is about $32,032 per year, though surveyors with the most education and experience could earn much more.

Ways of getting more information

School and public libraries should have books on the history and nature of surveying.

For more information, write to:

▶ American Congress on Surveying and Mapping
5410 Grosvenor Lane
Bethesda, MD 20814

▶ American Society for Photogrammetry and Remote Sensing
5410 Grosvenor Lane, Suite 210
Bethesda, MD 20814

Swimming-Pool Servicers

Other articles to look at:
- ▶ **General Maintenance Mechanics**
- ▶ **Heating and Cooling Technicians**
- ▶ **Janitors and Cleaners**
- ▶ **Plumbers**

What swimming-pool servicers do

Swimming-pool servicers take care of private and public swimming pools by cleaning, repairing, and maintaining them. They work with outdoor and indoor pools—in people's backyards, in neighborhood parks, and in health clubs and YMCAs.

Pools must be emptied of water at least once a year so that they may be thoroughly cleaned. Servicers will clean the sides and bottom of empty pools using detergent, brushes, heavy-duty vacuum cleaners, hoses, and sanding equipment. For outdoor pools, servicers must remove leaves and other debris from the top of the water using long-handled nets, usually on a daily basis.

When a swimming pool is filled with water, servicers will test the water on a regular basis to make sure it is clean and germ-free. They will add chemicals to the water to purify it. They must be careful to add the correct amount of each chemical, because if they don't add enough solution they may not kill all of the germs in the water.

In maintaining pools, servicers use equipment to adjust and make minor repairs to the pumping and heating equipment. They must clean and repair the filter system as well. After servicing a pool, workers write a report of the work performed. A copy of this report is given to the pool owner, and another copy is kept for the service company's files.

In areas with cold winters, outdoor swimming pools must be prepared and closed up for the cold months. Servicers remove equipment such as ladders and diving boards. They check all of the equipment to see whether anything needs to be fixed or replaced; they will either fix the items or have specialists fix them. The servicers then put the equipment in storage. Afterward, they drain the swimming pool and the filter. Then the entire pool is usually covered with waterproof canvas. If water is left in a pool over the winter, the water may freeze. Frozen water expands the sides of the pool and can crack or shatter the pool's frame.

Opening a pool in the spring involves many tasks. Servicers take the canvas cover off the pool. If the owner wishes, they may paint the inside of the pool. They take the ladders and other equipment out of storage and install this equipment. They start the system and look for problems such as leaks and they make any necessary repairs. Servicers fill the pool with water and make sure that the heating and circulation system is working properly. Finally, they add the necessary chemicals to the water. Some of the hardest physical labor for a swimming-pool servicer occurs during the set-up time in the spring.

Swimming-pool servicers work for companies located throughout the country. Some are employed by private pool owners, but most are employed by small companies. Larger companies may build and install pools in addition to servicing them.

Education and training

Swimming-pool servicers learn their skills on the job. They are trained by experienced employees. Many employers prefer workers with a high school diploma and they often hire people who are familiar with working with heating and cooling systems. Servicers must be licensed drivers because they have to travel to the pools they work on.

Earnings

The job outlook for swimming-pool servicers will be good in the 1990s as long as the number of swimming pools and hot tubs continues to grow. This will mean more work for new servicers. Also, as many workers leave their jobs, more job openings will be created for new and experienced pool servicers.

After completing their on-the-job training, pool servicers have earnings that range from about $9,600 to more than $12,000 per year. Servicers who have special skills or who work quickly may earn more than other workers. Some servicers earn additional money by working part-time with manufacturers and builders of swimming pools and in stores that stock swimming-pool equipment.

Ways of getting more information

The manager of a park district pool or your school pool may be able to help you contact a pool servicer so that you can find out more about what it's like to take care of swimming pools.

▶ A swimming-pool servicer nets debris that has blown into the pool during the night.

For more information write to the following organizations:

▶ National Spa and Pool Institute
  2111 Eisenhower Avenue
  Alexandria, VA 22314

▶ National Swimming Pool Foundation
  1083 Gulfdale, Suite 300
  San Antonio, TX 78216

Switchboard Operators

Other articles to look at:
► **Clerks**
► **Receptionists**
► **Telephone Operators**
► **Travel Agents**

What switchboard operators do

Switchboard operators handle the telephone calls that come into and go out of a business or office, as well as calls that go directly to a telephone company. There are two main types of switchboard operators: *central office operators* and *PBX operators*.

Central office operators work for a telephone company. They answer calls from people who want to know a phone number, or they connect calls that people want to make. Some of the operators in the central office are directory assistance operators. When someone calls asking for a person's number, they enter the name in a computer and the number appears on their screen. Central offices also employ long-distance operators. They handle collect calls, overseas calls, and conference calls. Pay-phone calls also go through the long-distance operator.

PBX stands for private branch exchange. More than half of all switchboard operators are PBX operators who work at the switchboards of private companies. When calls come into the company they answer them pleasantly, provide any information the caller may want, transfer calls to employees within the company, and take messages.

There are switchboard operators in many other areas, too. Operators in airports are called *communication center operators*. They page passengers and keep an eye on the airport's alarm system. *Police switchboard operators* take calls and pass information quickly to police officers. *Telephone answering services* have switchboard operators to take calls for people who pay to use the service.

Most switchboard operators work a standard 40-hour week. PBX operators usually work during regular business hours. Central office operators and those who work in 24-hour-a-day places such as hospitals and police stations may work evening or night shifts.

Education and training

Switchboard operators should have at least a high school education. High school courses in speech, mathematics, and business will be useful later as an operator. Telephone companies and private offices usually train their own operators on the job. New operators may be given several weeks of instruction before they begin on-the-job training. They learn how telephone switchboard equipment works and what the different telephone beeps and tones mean. They also listen to tapes of their own voices and practice to improve the way they sound, because switchboard operators should have pleasant, friendly voices.

Earnings

Job opportunities for switchboard operators are expected to increase throughout the

▶ Switchboard operators plug calls in to receiving phone lines.

1990s as businesses grow. However, the outlook for central office operators is expected to decline because of the new electronic and computer equipment that is taking over more and more tasks that people have done in the past. As with many other occupations, jobs for switchboard operators will open up as operators move on to other employment.

Operators who work for telephone companies usually earn more than do PBX operators. In the 1990s, the starting salaries for central office operators fell between $12,000 and $24,000 a year. PBX operators earned a salary of $12,000 to $18,000 per year.

Ways of getting more information

For more information write to the following agencies:

▶ Communications Workers of America
  1925 K Street, NW
  Washington, DC 20006

▶ United States Telephone Association
  900 19th Street, NW, Suite 800
  Washington, DC 20006

Systems Analysts

Other articles to look at:
- ▶ **Computer Operators**
- ▶ **Computer Programmers**
- ▶ **Computer-Service Technicians**
- ▶ **Mathematicians**
- ▶ **Scientific and Business Data-Processing Technicians**

What systems analysts do

Systems analysts help banks, government offices, and businesses of all kinds understand their computer systems. As more and more offices change from keeping records by hand to storing data in computers, analysts who can tailor computer systems and programs to the needs of a business, or even to the needs of just one department within a business, will become very important to any organization.

Systems analysts work with both the hardware and software parts of computer systems. The hardware includes the large items such as the computer itself, the monitor, and the keyboard; the software includes the computer programs, which are written and stored on diskettes, and the documentation (the manuals or guidebooks) that goes with the programs. Analysts design the best mix of hardware and software for the needs of the organization they are working for.

A systems analyst for the personnel department of a large company, for example, would first talk with the manager about what areas the computer could help with. The manager might be interested in knowing about how a new policy of giving employees longer paid vacations at Christmas has affected company profits for the month of December. The analyst can then show the manager what computer program to use, what data to enter, how to read the charts or graphs that the computer produces, and so on. The work of the analyst thus frees the manager to review the raw data—in this case, the numbers that show company profits were the same as in the previous Decembers—and decide how this information should affect company policy.

Once analysts have the computer system set up and running, they then advise on possible equipment and programming changes. Often, two or more people in a department each have their own computer, but they must be able to connect with and use information from others' computers. Analysts must then work with all the different computers in a department or an organization so the computers can connect with each other; this system of computers connecting with each other is called networking.

The areas analysts specialize in are as different as the businesses themselves; some deal with basic accounting while others help decide such complex questions as the flight path of a space shuttle.

Education and training

Almost all systems analysts have at least a bachelor's degree with majors in such subjects as computer science, mathematics, engineering, accounting, or business. Analysts going into specialized areas (aeronautics, for example) usually have graduate degrees as well.

In addition to a college degree, job experience as a computer programmer is very helpful. Many businesses hire systems analyst trainees from the ranks of their computer programmers. Systems analysts with several years of experience are often permitted into managerial jobs, especially as businesses find they need top staff members with an understanding of computers.

Earnings

This field is one of the fastest growing, and companies are always looking for qualified analysts, especially those with graduate degrees in computer science. Analysts are often in good positions to bargain for higher salaries or more benefits.

Average yearly earnings of systems analysts are about $35,800. Salaries for analysts in government are somewhat less than the average for private industry. Earnings also depend on years of experience and the type of business one works for.

Ways of getting more information

Many high schools offer classes in computer programming; this training helps in finding a part-time or summer job. Banks and insurance companies are often looking for students with some background in computers to work in data entry or programming while still in high school or college.

▶ Two systems analysts discuss the information path on a flow chart for their computer system.

For more information write to the following:

▶ Association for Systems Management
  1433 West Bagley Road
  Cleveland, OH 44138

▶ Data Processing Management Association
  505 Busse Highway
  Park Ridge, IL 60068

▶ Computer Science Association
  242 College Steet, 5th Floor
  Toronto, Ontario, Canada M5T 241

Tailors and Seamstresses

Other articles to look at:
▶ **Costume Designers**
▶ **Dry Cleaning and Laundry Workers**
▶ **Fashion Designers**
▶ **Knit Goods Industry Workers**

What tailors and seamstresses do

The *seamstress,* or *dressmaker,* and *tailor* sew custom-made clothing for men and women. Tailors construct tailored clothing, usually suits, jackets and coats; seamstresses or dressmakers usually construct women's clothing, including evening, wedding, and bridesmaid's gowns, and often women's suits as well.

Custom tailors or seamstresses may either make a garment from beginning to end, or, in larger shops, each employee may work on a specific task (such as measuring, cutting, fitting, or stitching) for each garment. Tailors and seamstresses also do alterations on ready-made clothing by measuring, cutting, and resewing it to fit the customer.

Custom tailors and seamstresses may be in business for themselves or may be employed by a small shop or the custom sections of large department stores. For alterations work, seamstresses and tailors are employed by retail clothing stores, including department stores, specialty stores, and bridal salons. They may also work for dry cleaning establishments.

When a person orders custom clothing, the tailor or seamstress first takes the customer's measurements, then cuts and sews together a sample garment from low-cost muslin fabric. This is fitted on the customer to be certain of a perfect fit before the expensive fabric is cut. The muslin garment is taken apart and used as a pattern to cut the finished garment, which is then sewn, brushed, and pressed. A final fitting is held before the customer takes the item home.

There is enormous satisfaction in creating a well-fitting piece of clothing for a grateful client. The tailor or seamstress needs not only superior sewing skills, but must also be able to interact with customers, some of whom have no idea how to sew (yet try to supervise the operation). They must be able to work quickly and accurately, because mistakes on expensive fabric can be costly, and time spent redoing the work wastes time and money as well.

Education and training

To become a seamstress or tailor, advanced training in the field of sewing and tailoring is necessary. Although these skills may be learned without benefit of any formal education or degrees, many employers prefer to hire college graduates with coursework in sewing, draping, pattern fitting, and design. Experience in the field is an advantage.

High school students interested in this field should take courses in home economics to get an idea of what is involved. If possible, it may be beneficial to take courses through area vocational or technical schools.

Apprenticeships may be available through custom tailor shops or garment manufacturing centers.

Earnings

Although some custom sewing jobs are likely to be lost through automation, openings for seamstresses and tailors should remain steady through the year 2000.

Those entering the career in manufacturing earn about $6.00 to $10.00 an hour. With experience, most seamstresses and tailors will earn between $18,000 to $30,000 per year; those at the top of their profession earn $52,000 or more per year.

Ways of getting more information

A visit to a department or clothing specialty store to observe a tailor or seamstress at work may be helpful in determining whether you would be interested in this type of career. For those high school students with the right skills, part-time jobs are sometimes available in those locations or in factories; or you may wish to offer your sewing services to friends and family to gain experience.

For more information about a career as a seamstress or tailor, write to the following:

▶ American Apparel Manufacturers Association
   2500 Wilson Boulevard, Suite 301
   Arlington, VA 22201

▶ Men's Fashion Association of America
   240 Madison Avenue
   New York, NY 10016

▶ New York Coat and Suit Association
   225 West 39th Street
   New York, NY 10122

▶ Correctly measuring a customer's clothing is an important part of accurately tailoring a suit.

Tax Preparers

Other articles to look at:
- ▶ **Accountants**
- ▶ **Auditors**
- ▶ **Bank Services Occupations**
- ▶ **Bookkeepers**
- ▶ **Insurance Policy Processing Occupations**

What tax preparers do

Tax preparers fill out tax forms and help people figure out how much money (if any) they owe in taxes. They use their knowledge of local, state, and national tax laws to ask tax-related questions, analyze important tax documents, and then complete tax returns for individuals and business firms.

To fill out tax forms, preparers meet with clients privately and look over all important tax documents. Preparers need to see wage statements, records of other income (like interest on a bank account), and any property tax information. Preparers often like to see a copy of the previous year's tax return. For most clients, especially business clients, it is also important to have an accurate listing of all business expenses (many business expenses are tax-deductible). Preparers then talk to the client to get additional information concerning their financial situation. They may ask questions about a client's investments or get details on how much the client spent on a business trip. Preparers must also be aware of any unusual profits or losses in a particular year. It is important to know, for example, if a client had large medical expenses or a great increase in the value of his or her stocks.

Once the financial information has been collected, tax preparers figure out how much taxes are owed and fill out the appropriate forms. If the tax return is relatively simple, the preparer will complete the return while the client waits. For more difficult returns (those requiring more calculations), the preparer will complete the forms at a later time. It can take several days for some returns.

Tax preparers must be very careful when doing tax calculations and determining what deductions a client is eligible for. Preparers use calculators and computers to check their results, and tax forms are always reviewed by another tax preparer to make sure they are accurate. Tax preparers must sign every tax form they complete and give a copy of the completed form to the client. Preparers always keep a record of all completed tax forms.

Tax preparers who work for tax service firms are often called *tax interviewers*. Most of their clients come to them during tax season, which is between January and mid-April. There are also a large number of tax preparers who are self-employed and work out of their homes.

Preparers must keep up with any changes in local, state, or federal tax laws. This requires constant study. Many tax companies sponsor review sessions each year during which time important tax law changes are discussed.

Education and training

Preparers must be able to work under deadline pressure and be able to work with all types of clients, including those who are nervous or upset about the taxes they may owe. The process of filling out tax forms can be very stressful for some clients and preparers must be able to handle these situations with tact and calm.

Although there are no specific educational requirements for this job, all preparers are high school graduates and most have at least some college training. Many preparers earn a college degree in business administration with an emphasis on taxes.

Most tax services provide new workers with on-the-job training during which time a new employee is carefully supervised. The new worker may spend several weeks or months reviewing the work of other preparers before working on actual tax situations. Most self-employed preparers have at least some work experience before starting their own tax-preparation business.

Earnings

As tax laws continue to become more complicated, more people will use the services of tax preparers. This should lead to good job opportunities for those in this field. Because most people need assistance between January and April of each year, many of these jobs will be part-time. During the tax season preparers may work as much as seven days a week, 11 hours a day.

Earnings often depend on how many tax returns a preparer can complete. Preparers can expect to earn between $50 and $150 a return depending on how complicated it is. Those who work for a tax service may have a set salary and get paid extra for each return they complete.

▶ A tax preparer checks a client's records while filling in the client's tax return forms.

Ways of getting more information

A good way to find out if you would enjoy being a tax preparer is to take a course in tax preparation or interview a preparer already working in the field.

In addition, write to the following organization and ask for information about being a tax preparer:

▶ National Association of Tax Practitioners
720 Association Drive
Appleton, WI 54914

Taxidermists

Other articles to look at:
▶ **Archaeologists**
▶ **Biologists**
▶ **Museum Curators**
▶ **Naturalists**
▶ **Veterinarians**

What taxidermists do

Taxidermists prepare, stuff, and mount the skins of birds, fish, and other animals to create lifelike models. Some of these models are trophies for hunters. Others are created for museum exhibits.

Taxidermists begin their work by skinning the animal they are preparing. They do this work with special knives, scissors, and pliers. Once the skin is removed, it is preserved with chemical solutions.

Then the taxidermists create a foundation meant to resemble the skeleton of the animal. The foundation is made with materials that include clay, plaster, burlap, papier mâché, wire mesh, and glue. After the foundation has been created, the preserved skin is attached with adhesives or modeling clay. Finally, the eyes, teeth, and claws are attached. In the case of the eyes, taxidermists often use glass or plastic replicas because it is difficult to preserve the original tissue.

Taxidermists work with a variety of subjects, including large game animals, such as elk and bears, birds, fish, and reptiles. Usually, taxidermists create a model of the entire animal. Sometimes, however, they only model the head. This is often true of large animals, especially those with impressive antlers. And sometimes taxidermists will only preserve the skin of an animal. Such skins are often used as rugs.

Museums often call on taxidermists to create models of animals that are extinct. In such cases, the taxidermists work from detailed drawings and paintings of animals. They use natural and artificial furs, teeth, claws, and feathers to create a model that looks as much as possible like the extinct animal must have looked.

Natural science museums also use taxidermists to create dioramas, which are the displays that show animals in their habitats. Animals are donated or obtained from zoos, parks, or other places when the animal dies from natural causes. After the veterinarian determines the cause of death, the taxidermist comes in to prepare the animal for display.

The animal is set in a display with a wall painting behind it and plants and other items around it that would be found in its home in nature. This creates a sense of what the animal's natural environment is; this may be the only way that most people get to see types of rare animals.

Education and training

Taxidermists must have artistic ability, a good knowledge of animal anatomy, and special training in taxidermy processes. High school

▶ A taxidermist fills a fish with stuffing to keep the fish's shape.

students should take courses in art, biology, and wood and metal shop. After high school, students can attend one of eight schools in the United States that offer courses in taxidermy.

Earnings

Beginning taxidermists often earn just the minimum wage. Experienced taxidermists average about $14,000 per year. Museum workers may earn $20,000 a year or more, but they usually have other duties in addition to their taxidermy work.

Ways of getting more information

You can get more information about a career as a taxidermist by writing to the following:

▶ National Taxidermists Association
   18626 St. Clair Avenue
   Cleveland, OH 44110

▶ North American Institute of Taxidermy
   2408 Penn Avenue North
   Minneapolis, MN 55411

▶ Southland School of Taxidermy
   2603 Osceola Street
   Baton Rouge, LA 70805

Teacher Aides

Other articles to look at:
► **Child Care Center Workers**
► **Elementary School Teachers**
► **In-House Child Care Workers**
► **Secondary School Teachers**

What teacher aides do

Teachers must plan and teach lessons, grade papers, prepare exams, attend faculty meetings, and perform other duties around the school. *Teacher aides* take care of some of the more routine school tasks and thus free the teacher to spend more time preparing for and teaching classes.

The duties of a teacher aide include preparing some instructional materials, helping students with classroom work, and supervising lunchrooms, playgrounds, and other areas around and within the school. Some teacher aides also do administrative paperwork, grade tests, and operate audiovisual equipment.

Some teacher aides work directly in the classroom. They may take attendance and distribute materials such as books, photocopies, and writing supplies. They also set up and operate slide and film projectors, tape recorders and phonographs, and VCRs.

Teacher aides also work outside of the classroom. They may be in charge of keeping order in the cafeteria, the library, and hallways, as well as in the playground. They might also make sure students get on the correct school bus.

Assisting teachers with clerical chores is an important part of being a teacher aide. For example, aides may help teachers by doing filing, typing, and photocopying. They also may fill out request forms for classroom supplies.

In some schools, teacher aides may even do some teaching. The aides may lecture, conduct group discussions, or listen to elementary school children read. Aides may take charge of school projects, such as science fairs. Often, aides will take students on field trips to such places as museums and zoos.

Teacher aides work at all levels of education. Although they are most often found in elementary schools, teacher aides also work in high schools and even at some colleges and universities. At the college level, teacher aides are often graduate students and are called *teaching assistants,* or *TAs.*

Education and training

Educational requirements for teacher aides depend on the type of work the aides will be doing. Teacher aides who handle just clerical or supervisory duties may need only a high school diploma. Sometimes, even a high school education is not required. If the aides will be doing any teaching or classroom work, however, some college work is usually required. Sometimes a college degree is necessary.

Teacher aides often receive on-the-job training, usually under the supervision of a certified teacher.

▶ A day-care worker teaches children how to prepare a snack.

Earnings

The need for teacher aides is expected to increase about as fast as average during the 1990s. The relatively high turnover in this career should result in openings to replace those workers who retire or go on to other occupations or become full-time teachers.

Salaries for teacher aides vary with geographic location, the academic qualifications of the aide, and the duties performed. Teacher aides performing nonteaching duties usually earn about $6.14 per hour. Aides with some teaching duties average about $7.05 per hour.

Ways of getting more information

Interested students can get more information about a career as a teacher aide by writing to the following organization:

▶ American Federation of Teachers
555 New Jersey Avenue NW
Washington, DC 20001

Technical Writers

Other articles to look at:
▶ **Book Editors**
▶ **Computer Programmers**
▶ **Magazine Editors**
▶ **Scientific and Business Data-Processing Technicians**
▶ **Writers and Authors**

What technical writers do

Technical writers put scientific and technical information into easily understandable language. They prepare service manuals, sales literature, catalogs, and other instructional materials used by salespeople to sell various types of equipment. This instructional material is also used by technicians who install, maintain, and repair the equipment. Many writers develop instructional guides for users of home computers. Occasionally, technical writers assist in the preparation of speeches, articles, and other scientific papers.

Before technical writers begin a project, they must have a thorough understanding of the subject they are writing about. Before creating literature on a computer system or other product, for example, they study reports, journal articles, engineering drawings, and other materials that explain in detail how a product is built and how it works. Writers also talk to engineers, scientists, and other specialists who have a good background in the development of a particular product. After this research, the writer might observe the product being made to see firsthand how the various parts are put together.

After collecting enough background information, the writer is ready to begin writing. A service manual will often require more detail than a sales catalog, but all materials require a clear writing style that fully explains how a product works. Some writers arrange for the preparation of graphs, charts, and other artwork to illustrate how a product works.

After a first draft has been prepared, the technical writer will ask engineers and other people familiar with the product to read the material to make sure that it is accurate and understandable. The engineers' comments help the writer find out if there is a need for additional information or to change the style or content of the material.

Education and training

Technical writers must be able to express their ideas clearly and logically. They should be able to present the information in a creative way and also have the discipline to complete a project on time. Writers should be familiar with research techniques and have an understanding of how computers operate.

Most technical writers start their careers as scientists, engineers, or technicians. Some writers begin as research assistants in a company's technical information department. The best way to become a technical writer is to have a bachelor's degree in a specialized field such as engineering or business. Courses in English and composition are also necessary.

▶ Technical writers confer with the scientist on how to best explain an aspect of the work the scientist is doing.

Earnings

Because of the increasing need to communicate scientific and technical information to salespeople, researchers, and others, technical writers should find good job opportunities in the 1990s. But, as is the case with all jobs in the writing field, there will be a great deal of competition for these jobs.

Salaries for technical writers range between $19,800 and $46,300 per year. Those who earn $40,000 or more annually often have many years of experience.

Ways of getting more information

A good way to find out if you would enjoy being a technical writer is to work on a school newspaper or gain other writing experience.

In addition, write to the following:

▶ Society for Technical Communication
901 North Stuart Street, Suite 304
Arlington, VA 22203

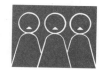

Telecommunications Technicians

Other articles to look at:
- ► **Cable-Television Technicians**
- ► **Communications Equipment Mechanics**
- ► **Electronics Technicians**
- ► **Telephone Installers and Repairers**

What telecommunications technicians do

Telecommunications technicians install, maintain, and repair a wide variety of telecommunications equipment, which is used for transmitting voices and data across distances. Telecommunications systems are typically used to link telephones, but they may also link computers, fax machines, or teletype machines. Most telecommunications technicians work in telephone company offices or wherever telephone customers need equipment installed or repaired.

Other kinds of equipment are also used in telecommunications. Messages and signals can be sent using telegraph wires, laser beams, microwave transmissions, satellites, and fiber optics cables. Often several kinds of equipment are linked together in a complicated system. The following paragraphs describe a few of the many technicians who work in this complex industry.

Central office technicians and *switching equipment technicians* work in telephone company central offices. They install, test, repair, and maintain the equipment that automatically connects lines when customers dial.

PBX systems technicians work on PBXs (private branch exchanges), which are direct lines that businesses install to bypass telephone company lines. PBX equipment can provide specialized services like electronic mail and automatic routing of calls at the lowest possible cost.

Submarine cable equipment technicians work with machines and equipment used to send messages through underwater cables. Working in cable offices and stations, they check on transmitters and printers and replace faulty parts.

Automatic-equipment technicians work for telegraph companies, maintaining and adjusting telegraph equipment. *Network control technicians* work with electronic networks transmitting data that use several different kinds of equipment, such as a combination of telephone lines, satellites, and computers. They electronically test the various parts of the network and monitor its performance in operation.

Microwave technicians help design, test, and install various parts of microwave communications systems and radar equipment. Most of these technicians are employed by the army and other defense industries.

Education and training

Telecommunications employers prefer to hire technicians who have already learned the necessary skills, which can be done either through service in the military or from a post–high school training program, such as those available at community and junior colleges or vocational institutes. These schools offer programs in telecommunications technology, computer maintenance, electronics, and other appropriate subjects.

While in high school, students who are thinking about entering this field should take algebra, geometry, physics, and computer courses. They should take shop courses that introduce them to principles of electricity and electronics. Students should also take English courses that help to develop language skills needed for reading instructional manuals and writing reports.

Earnings

Job opportunities for telecommunications technicians are expected to decline during the 1990s. Increasing computerization in the telephone industry is expected to greatly reduce the need for technicians who provide routine maintenance and repair services. On the other hand, employment in some areas of telecommunications is growing as computer technology changes and as equipment becomes increasingly complex. The demand for qualified microwave technicians, for example, should be very strong for the foreseeable future. In general, technicians who have the best training will be best able to get good jobs as new technology emerges.

The earnings of telecommunications technicians vary widely depending on the nature of their duties, level of experience, geographic location, and their employer. Some central office and PBX installers receive an annual salary of $33,800. Mechanics generally earn less than PBX installers and central office workers.

▶ With the wiring from a major phone line hookup, a telecommunications technician adds a connector to the lines that send calls to the main cable.

Ways of getting more information

With the help of a teacher or guidance counselor, students may be able to arrange a visit to a local telephone company to see technicians on the job and to talk with them.

In addition, students can write to the following organizations for more information:

▶ Communications Workers of America
  1925 K Street, NW
  Washington, DC 20006

▶ United States Telephone Association
  900 19th Street, NW, Suite 800
  Washington, DC 20006

Telemarketers

Other articles to look at:
▶ **Advertising Sales Workers**
▶ **Marketing Researchers**
▶ **Public Relations Specialists**
▶ **Receptionists**
▶ **Telephone Operators**

What telemarketers do

Telemarketers sell goods and services on the telephone. They also take orders, handle complaints, and conduct surveys. Their skills at dealing with the public on the phone are of great use to many different kinds of businesses.

Many stores and manufacturers have toll-free 800 numbers, and they encourage customers to use the phone to ask questions or make complaints. Some stores don't have retail outlets but instead sell all of their products through catalogs. Telemarketing offices for these businesses often take customers' calls as they come in, seven days a week, 24 hours a day.

Telemarketers are employed either by the firm selling the goods or services or by an agency that sells the services of its telemarketers for limited periods of time. Some agencies work in one particular field. For example, an agency may specialize in fund-raising or in book or magazine promotions.

Telemarketers make outgoing calls and receive incoming calls. The outgoing calls are usually to persons who returned a reply card or who have shown some interest in a product. Sometimes telemarketers make calls to potential customers chosen at random—these are called cold calls. When telemarketers make these calls they usually deliver a prepared message.

Telemarketers who take inbound calls not only accept orders for various products but also do such other jobs as making airplane reservations, selling tickets to concerts or ball games, and giving out various kinds of information.

Many telemarketers work in offices, usually at the company or agency headquarters. They might make their calls in an office with four or five other workers or in a room with several hundred. Some companies employ telemarketers who work out of their own homes, usually during the evening hours.

Education and training

Most telemarketing centers and agencies want persons with at least a high school diploma, and some firms hire only college graduates. Classes that help prepare students for this field are speech, drama, English, and business.

Telemarketers usually receive a great deal of on-the-job training. Companies or agencies that hire telemarketers have instructors on their staffs who show new employees how to use the equipment and how to read the scripts. They teach them sales techniques and listening skills. Instructors advise train-

▶ A telemarketer calls one of the people on her contact list.

ees on how to calm angry customers and how to respond to complaints.

Those who would like to work in this field should have patience and, especially, a good attitude. Telemarketers often must deal with rude customers, and they must always remain courteous.

Earnings

Telemarketing is expected to continue to be a field with many opportunities.

In the 1990s, part-time employees making simple calls earned between minimum wage and $8.00 per hour. Telemarketers making

business-to-business calls can make between $17,000 and $30,000 per year.

Ways of getting more information

For more information write to the following:

▶ American Marketing Association
250 South Wacker Drive, Suite 200
Chicago, IL 60606

Telephone Installers and Repairers

Other articles to look at:
▶ **Communications Equipment Mechanics**
▶ **Electrical Technicians**
▶ **Electricians**
▶ **Line Installers and Cable Splicers**
▶ **Telecommunications Technicians**

What telephone installers and repairers do

Telephone installers and *telephone repairers* put in, take out, service, and repair telephones in homes and offices. Sometimes the jobs of the telephone installer and the telephone repairer are combined, and the worker is called a *telephone installer-repairer.*

Whenever customers request a new telephone, add an extension, or replace an old wall telephone, installers do all the necessary work. They travel to the customer's home or office in a truck that contains all the needed equipment. If the customer needs a new connection to the central telephone office, installers climb a nearby telephone pole to attach the incoming wire to the service line. On some jobs, they bore through walls and floors to do the necessary wiring. In addition to home and business telephones, installers also put in telephone booths and coin collectors.

Sometimes wear and tear of wires and parts causes a telephone to work improperly. When this happens, it is the job of the telephone repairer to test the phone, locate the trouble, and fix the problem.

Some stores, business offices, hotels, and other buildings have a single telephone number. However, to channel the large number of incoming and outgoing calls, businesses use a switchboard system. This is like having a private telephone system (called a private branch exchange, or PBX) within the building. A *PBX installer* sets up the necessary wiring and switchboard equipment to make the system function. Some PBX installers also set up teletypewriters, mobile radiophones, and equipment for television and radio broadcasting. And, like regular telephone repairers, *PBX repairers* locate any troubles with a PBX system and then repair them. The *PBX installer-repairer* has the combined jobs of PBX installer and PBX repairer.

Education and training

Telephone companies like to hire inexperienced persons and train them for telephone and PBX installation and repair jobs. However, to be considered for a telephone training program, applicants must be high school or vocational school graduates who like working with their hands and have a fair amount of mechanical ability.

Once hired, new workers must complete a seven-month training program that combines on-the-job work experience with formal classroom instruction. After workers have become qualified telephone installers, additional training is necessary before they can become tele-

▶ A telephone installer checks the new telephone lines from the stadium press box.

phone repairers, PBX installers, or PBX repairers.

Earnings

Job opportunities for telephone installers and repairers are expected to decline in the 1990s. It has become easier than in the past for people to purchase telephones at stores and install them by themselves. Also, repairs are not needed as often anymore because it is almost just as expensive to have equipment repaired as it is to buy new items.

Salaries for installers and repairers vary with experience and geographic location. Some workers earn an average yearly salary of about $33,000. It usually takes about five years for a worker to advance from a beginning pay rate to a top pay rate.

Ways of getting more information

Building electronic kits or putting together model airplanes or cars are ways to test your mechanical inclinations and ability to work with your hands and follow drawings and plans.

For more information write to:

▶ Communications Workers of America
    1925 K Street, NW
    Washington, DC 20006

▶ International Brotherhood of Electrical Workers
    1125 15th Street, NW
    Washington, DC 20005

Telephone Operators

Other articles to look at:
- ▶ **Clerks**
- ▶ **Radio and Telegraph Operators**
- ▶ **Receptionists**
- ▶ **Reservation and Transportation Ticket Agents**
- ▶ **Travel Agents**

What telephone operators do

Telephone operators help customers complete telephone calls and answer customer inquiries for telephone numbers. They may also help customers who have difficulty in dialing or those in emergency situations. Telephone operators are always available to answer calls, 24 hours a day and seven days a week.

Telephone company operators usually work in large central offices. They wear headsets that contain both an earphone and a microphone, leaving their hands free to operate the switchboard or, more often now, the computer terminal in front of which they are seated. Operators provide customers with a variety of services. They help customers with collect calls, long-distance calls, and other connections that require assistance. In these instances, they obtain the information needed to complete the call and record the details for billing. *Directory assistance operators* obtain telephone numbers for customers by using telephone directories that have alphabetical and geographic listings. Upon finding the telephone number, the directory assistance oper-

ator will read the number to the customer or will activate a computerized recording that provides the customer with the number.

Although most people are familiar with the operators that work for telephone companies, there are also operators that work for other types of companies. These operators, called *PBX operators,* transfer incoming calls to the correct person, give information to callers, assist employees in making calls, and record charges for outgoing calls.

Education and training

Telephone operators should be pleasant, courteous, and have nice speaking voices. They should also not mind sitting for long periods of time. Operators must be good listeners and have good reading skills and legible handwriting. Good hand-to-eye coordination and an ability to work under pressure are also important.

There are no specific educational requirements for this job, but most employers prefer to hire high school graduates. New operators are given one to three weeks of individual training under the supervision of an experienced operator. During this time they are taught how to handle the different types of calls and any emergency situations. Operators are then assigned to a regular position at the switchboard. They continue to receive on-the-job training as more modern equipment becomes available.

▶ Telephone operators check telephone number listings on computers.

Earnings

Although telephone operators will continue to find fairly good job opportunities in the near future, computers and other types of automated equipment will decrease the number of operators needed. Private companies will continue to hire a large number of PBX operators, but large telephone companies may reduce the number of operators they hire.

The wages paid to operators vary from state to state and even from city to city. Yearly salaries are usually between $15,600 and $25,400. Those who work for telephone companies usually belong to unions and earn somewhat more than those who work for private companies.

Ways of getting more information

A good way to find out if you would enjoy being a full-time telephone operator is to get a part-time or summer job as a receptionist. In addition, write to the following organizations:

▶ Communications Workers of America
  1925 K Street, NW
  Washington, DC 20006

▶ United States Telephone Association
  900 19th Street, NW, Suite 800
  Washington, DC 20006

Textile Technicians

What textile technicians do

Textile technicians work with engineers and designers to make different kinds of cloth and cloth products. Blankets and automobile seat belts, parachutes and bandages—these and so many other items are all made of textiles. This field splits into two industries: the textile industry, which produces cloth, and the apparel industry, which produces clothing. Technicians are also called *apparel manufacturing technicians.*

In the textile industry, some technicians work on developing new kinds of yarn or thread. They work with natural fibers, such as wool and cotton, and with man-made materials, such as polyester and rayon. Sometimes they take a piece of fabric and figure out what fibers are in it and how it was made. Then they can decide how to improve it. For example, textile technicians have helped make flame-resistant cloth for fire fighters' coats and bacteria-resistant cloth for hospital gowns.

Both textile and apparel technicians may work in manufacturing. These technicians need to understand the complicated machines that carry out many manufacturing processes. They need to learn management and speaking skills so that they can train workers to operate machines. They also may program computers to operate some machines.

Technicians in manufacturing may have to know how long each step of production takes, exactly what material is needed, and how the product will move from one process to another. For example, an apparel manufacturing technician may have to plan the cutting of fabric into pieces or the sewing of those pieces into a garment.

Other textile and apparel technicians work in laboratories testing the quality of the manufactured goods. These quality-control technicians test cloth for strength, thickness, wrinkle resistance, color, and other things. In the apparel industry, technicians check garments for size, construction, and appearance.

Education and training

Textile technicians need to complete high school and take at least two years of further training at a technical school or a community college. High school students interested in becoming textile technicians should study English, at least two years of mathematics, and science courses that involve laboratory work. Courses in computers and mechanical drafting are also useful.

Two-year degree programs that should be taken include science, mathematics, English, and computer programming. Students who

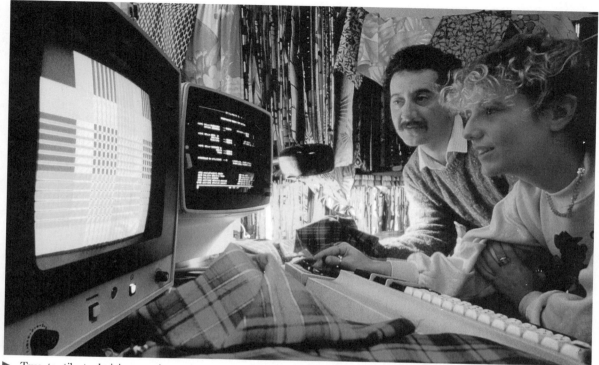

▶ Two textile technicians register the color of each strand to be woven into a cloth on a machine weaver.

are interested in the textile industry will learn about fibers, the processes of making yarn and fabric, and methods of testing textiles.

Earnings

Overall growth in the textile industry will be slow; however, the demand for technicians who know how to work with computers and advanced machinery will increase.

Beginning textile technicians earn between $14,000 and $20,000. With four to six years of work experience, textile technicians earn up to $25,000 a year. Jobs in the apparel industry pay somewhat more than jobs in the textile industry. With increased experience and responsibility, technicians' salaries can go up to $40,000 or more.

Ways of getting more information

Visiting a textile or apparel factory, if there are any nearby, would be a good way to learn about how cloth or clothing is made.

For more information write to the following organizations:

▶ National Council for Textile Education
PO Box 391
Charlottesville, VA 22902

▶ Canadian Textiles Institute
280 Albert Street, Suite 502
Ottawa, Ontario, Canada K1P 5G8

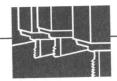

Textile Workers

Other articles to look at:
▶ **Industrial Machinery Mechanics**
▶ **Knit Goods Industry Workers**
▶ **Leather Tanning and Finishing Workers**
▶ **Machinists**
▶ **Textile Technicians**

What textile workers do

Many of the products we use, from the clothes we wear to the rugs we walk on, are made from textiles (woven fabrics). *Textile workers* are people involved with converting natural and manufactured fibers into usable products. Some workers operate machinery that makes the fiber and yarn used to produce fabrics; others are employed in the areas of design, research, and marketing. A worker's specific responsibilities depend on the area in which he or she works.

The textile manufacturing process begins with the preparation of manufactured or natural fibers for spinning. Operators oversee machines that break up large quantities of fibers, remove some of the damaged fibers, and blend the rest of the fibers together into spools of yarn. This yarn is then fastened onto other machines where it is woven together with other fabric to produce various products. While the machines are in operation, operators replace spools of yarn as needed and watch for any problems, such as yarn breaking or new needles needing to be put on.

The fibers are then woven into large sheets of materials. The material may be plain or patterned. Some workers set the looms up; others make sure the pattern is developing correctly.

Workers are also needed in other areas of the production process. They clean and wash the fabric after it has gone through the spinning machines, and many fabrics are dyed with color or given special finishes that make them waterproof or wrinkle-resistant.

After the production process, workers inspect the fabrics to make sure there are no flaws, iron the material, and box the finished product for shipping.

Other workers involved in the textile industry include the designers, who create patterns and then choose the colors and yarn to make those patterns; production managers, who supervise the making of the garments and keep track of costs and other important work records; and machine repair personnel, who fix any major problems and do maintenance tasks such as greasing and oiling the machines to prevent problems from occurring.

Education and training

The best way to become a textile worker is to complete an apprenticeship program offered by textile manufacturers. These programs range from several months to several years in duration and combine on-the-job training with courses in mathematics and machine shop practice. Many community colleges and technical schools also offer two-year programs in textile making.

▶ Watching a bolt of material being printed, a textile worker checks for quality of the design printed on the material.

Earnings

With the increased use of automated machinery and the increased competition from foreign textile companies, employment opportunities for textile workers are expected to continue to decline during the 1990s. Most of the new workers will be hired to replace those who retire or stop working in this industry for other reasons.

The average salary for production workers is about $14,000 per year. Those who work late evening shifts may earn somewhat more than this. Supervisors and other managerial personnel should earn about $20,000 annually.

Ways of getting more information

For more information, write to the following:

▶ American Textile Manufacturers Institute
   1801 K Street, NW
   Washington, DC 20006

▶ Canadian Textiles Institute
   280 Albert Street, Suite 502
   Ottawa, Ontario, Canada K1P 5G8

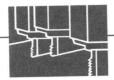

Tire Technicians

Other articles to look at:
► **Automobile Mechanics**
► **Plastics Products Manufacturing Workers**
► **Plastics Technicians**
► **Quality-Control Technicians**
► **Rubber Goods Production Workers**

What tire technicians do

Tire technicians work for tire companies, testing tires to find out how strong the tires are, how long they will last, and whether there are any flaws in their construction. Sometimes they test experimental models of tires that are not yet ready for manufacturing, and sometimes they test samples of finished tires as they come out of the factory. Technicians who are involved mostly with testing tires from the factory are called *quality-control technicians.*

In order to carry out testing procedures, tire technicians inflate the tires and mount them on machines that re-create the stresses of actual road conditions, such as traveling at high speeds, carrying heavy loads, going over bumpy roads, and skidding in wet weather. The technicians can adjust the machines to change the speed or the weight of the load or the bumpiness of the road surface. Then, either while the tire is on the machine or after it is taken off, they use pressure gauges and other devices that detect whether any parts of the tire are damaged. They continue testing the tire until it fails or until it has lasted for some specified period of time.

Another kind of testing that tire technicians do involves cutting cross sections from brand-new or road-tested tires. Technicians use power saws to cut up tires and then inspect the pieces for the condition of the plies (which are rubbery sheets of material inside the tire) and the tread (which is the part of the tire that makes contact with the road). Treads must be checked carefully to see that the indentations, or cords, on them are good enough for gripping the road.

Throughout the testing, tire technicians keep careful records of all test results. Later, they prepare reports that sometimes include charts, tables, and graphs to help describe and explain the results of the tests.

Education and training

Tire technicians need to be high school graduates. For some jobs, employers prefer applicants who have training in a field related to manufacturing or product testing. This kind of training may be received at a vocational school or a community or junior college.

While in high school, students interested in this career should take courses in science and mathematics, including algebra and geometry, and English courses that improve their reading and writing skills. They should also take shop or laboratory science courses that introduce them to measuring devices, electrical machinery, and electronic testing equipment.

Earnings

It is difficult to forecast future employment opportunities for tire technicians. Employment levels in the tire industry are very much tied to the number of new cars being sold, and it is possible that the number of new cars manufactured and sold in this country will decrease in coming years. In addition, tire makers in the United States face competition from foreign tire manufacturers, so that production in this country could decline. If that happens, there will be fewer jobs for tire technicians.

Salaries for tire technicians vary depending on the kind of testing they do, how much supervision they require, and how much training they have had. Some skilled and experienced technicians who can work with little supervision earn $30,000 to $36,000 a year. Technicians with little experience and no training after high school may make around $14,000 to $18,000 per year, although some may earn less. Most tire technicians make between $18,000 and $30,000 each year.

Ways of getting more information

Students can explore their interest in similar work through shop or laboratory science courses in which they operate machinery or make precise measurements with mechanical or electronic equipment.

In addition, students can write to the following organizations for more information about working as a tire technician:

▶ Checking the wear on the tire after a stress test, a technician measures the tread of a tractor tire.

▶ American Society for Quality Control
  310 West Wisconsin Avenue
  Milwaukee, WI 53203

▶ International Tire Association
  PO Box 1067
  Farmington, CT 06034

Title Searchers and Examiners

Other articles to look at:
- ▶ **Assessors and Appraisers**
- ▶ **Lawyers**
- ▶ **Legal Assistants**
- ▶ **Librarians**
- ▶ **Real Estate Agents and Brokers**

What title searchers and examiners do

In the real estate business (the buying and selling of buildings and land), a title refers to the legal right of ownership of property. When a house or piece of land is sold, the buyer receives title to it from the seller. But before the right of ownership passes from the seller to the buyer, a title search and examination is usually done. This is the work of *title searchers* and *title examiners*.

The purpose of a title search and examination is to make sure that the seller has clear title to the property. Title searchers begin by reading the search request. They find out what type of title evidence is required. They note the legal description of the property and the names of the people involved. Then, they begin the actual title search.

The title search is done using public and private records. These records list mortgages, deeds, and other legal documents that can affect the title to a property. They also compare the legal description in the title request with the one shown in the records. This allows time to check the deed of ownership and the description of the property's boundaries. Title searchers may request drawings showing the boundaries of the property.

Title searchers also list transactions (business dealings) related to the property. For example, the owner may have hired a worker to install a new patio. If the owner did not pay the worker, he or she may have filed a lien against the property. A lien is a claim on property for an unpaid debt. Liens must be removed (paid off) to clear the title to a property. Title searchers also check tax records to make sure the owner has paid his or her taxes. If taxes are owed, they must be paid before clear title can pass to the new owner of the property.

Title examiners go over the information collected by title searchers. They decide whether the owner of a property has clear title to it. In doing so, they study copies of various records, including mortgages, liens, and deeds. Examiners also check records of legal matters that can affect title to a property. These include births, marriages, and divorces. If the owner does not have clear title, examiners list what the owner needs to do to clear the title. Some title examiners work for title insurance companies. After they complete a title examination, they may prepare a title insurance policy. Such a policy guarantees that the seller has legal title to the property being sold.

It is important for both the buyer and the seller to make sure that the sale of the property is legal and the new owner has the title legally.

▶ Title searchers check on property rights to a lot being purchased by a client.

Education and training

Title searchers and examiners are employed by title insurance companies, government offices, and law firms. Many of these workers are given on-the-job training. Most employers expect job seekers to have a high school diploma, and they look for people who can read quickly and who have clear handwriting. In many states, licenses or certificates are required for title searchers and examiners.

Earnings

The job outlook for these workers is expected to be fair. Jobs are most plentiful when the real estate market is strong. Salaries of experienced title searchers range from $11,000 to about $15,000 per year.

Ways of getting more information

Although finding work in a title company's office may be difficult for a student, experience working in a bank or a real estate firm could be valuable.

For more information about the work of title searchers and examiners, write to the following agency:

▶ American Land Title Association
   1828 L Street, NW, Suite 705
   Washington, DC 20036

Tobacco Products Industry Workers

Other articles to look at:
► **Agricultural Equipment Technicians**
► **Assemblers**
► **Canning Industry Workers**
► **Farm Crop Production Technicians**
► **Food Production Workers**

What tobacco products industry workers do

Tobacco products industry workers are involved with making cigars, cigarettes, chewing tobacco, smoking tobacco, and snuff. These products are made from leaf tobacco, which grows from plants. Workers dry, cure, age, cut, roll, form, and package various products.

Workers first harvest the tobacco. Then the tobacco is cured or dried. Workers separate the tobacco leaves from the stems. This is done either by hand or by feeding the cured tobacco into machines. Then the tobacco is dried again by *redrying-machine operators,* who use machines equipped with hot air and fans.

After redrying, the tobacco is aged by sprinkling it with water. *Bulkers* and *prizers* then pack, or prize, the tobacco into barrels called hogsheads. *Hydraulic-press operators* pack hogsheads using scales, electric hoists, and hydraulic presses.

After the tobacco has been aged, *blenders* mix together various kinds of tobacco to produce a blend with certain characteristics. After blending, some tobacco is flavored with what is called casing fluid. Casing workers prepare the fluid, soak the tobacco with it, and then remove the excess fluid.

Now the tobacco is ready to be cut. Workers feed the tobacco into shredding machines. Some of the shredded tobacco is ground into a product called snuff, which is pulverized tobacco. Cut tobacco is fed into machines that manufacture cigarettes and cigars. Some cigars are made by hand. Machines also form tobacco into shapes that are called plugs, lumps, and twists. This type of tobacco is chewed. Workers then pack the tobacco products for shipping.

Also important to the tobacco industry are *product inspectors*. These workers are responsible for assuring the quality of tobacco products.

Education and training

No formal education is required for most tobacco products industry jobs. A grade school diploma is usually sufficient. Workers learn their skills on the job. Maintenance and mechanical workers may need a high school diploma and machine maintenance experience or skills.

Earnings

Employment of tobacco industry workers is expected to remain steady in the 1990s.

▶ At an auction, tobacco products industry workers examine different lots of tobacco produced.

However, because of the efforts of health care professionals, Americans appear to be more aware of the dangers of tobacco and as a result jobs in this industry are expected to slowly decline.

In the 1990s, cigarette makers earned about $23,000 a year. Cigar workers earned less, and skilled workers earned more. In general, salaries depend on plant size, plant location, and the level of the worker's skills.

Ways of getting more information

For more information about a career as a tobacco products industry worker write to the following organizations:

▶ Bakery, Confectionery and Tobacco Workers International Union
   10401 Connecticut Avenue
   Kensington, MD 20895

▶ Cigar Association of America, Inc.
   1100 17th Street, NW
   Washington, DC 20036

▶ Tobacco Growers' Information Committee
   PO Box 12300
   Raleigh, NC 27605

Toll Collectors

Other articles to look at:
► **Bank Services Occupations**
► **Border Patrol Officers**
► **Cashiers**
► **Clerks**
► **Reservation and Transportation Ticket Agents**

What toll collectors do

The U.S. economy depends on the huge, crisscrossing web of roads, bridges, and tunnels that spreads across the country. Without this interconnecting system of transportation, people couldn't travel from state to state, workers couldn't get to and from work, and goods couldn't get from farm to factory or from stockroom to store. But because the cost of building and maintaining the system is high, many roads, bridges, tunnels, and even ferry boats charge a fee, or toll, to the people who use them. The workers who collect these fees are called *toll collectors*.

Toll collectors perform a wide range of duties. First and foremost, they collect fees from vehicles passing through their toll stations. The rates vary according to the size or weight of the vehicle, so collectors must be aware of all the various rates possible. They make change, count and sort the money they receive, fill out bank deposit slips, and keep written records on the amount of traffic and kinds of vehicles that pass through their station.

In addition to handling the financial end of toll collecting, these workers give directions to travelers, pass on messages received through their radio equipment, and notify state police, ambulances, or other emergency services when necessary. They may monitor the automatic lanes (the exact-change lanes where motorists just toss their toll money into a basket), check for unsafe or prohibited vehicles on the roadway, and make sure the equipment at their station is working properly.

Toll collectors work around the clock, every day of the year. Their busiest shifts are usually on holidays, evenings, and weekends. Still, most collectors enjoy their work. They come in contact with all kinds of people every day, and they have the satisfaction of knowing that their courtesy and friendliness give travelers a lasting impression of the thruway network as a whole.

Education and training

Toll collectors should have at least a high school education, and those wishing to rise up the management ranks should have some college experience as well. People who have worked as cashiers will have an advantage over other applicants, but no previous training is required. Any experience in handling money and making change will be valuable in this career. All would-be collectors must take an exam before being hired; they are tested on their ability to deal with the public, make

▶ Toll collectors receive the money paid by drivers when they use a toll bridge or road.

change and handle other financial transactions, and keep records and write reports.

Earnings
Salaries vary from state to state, but on the average, beginning toll collectors earn about $11,500 a year, while more experienced collectors earn up to $19,000 a year. Those employees with the education, experience, and work skills to go into management may earn anywhere from $21,000 to $45,000 a year.

Ways of getting more information
Interested students can talk to people at the state job service office or toll authority about the exact responsibilities of toll collectors.

For more information write to:

▶ American Association of State Highway and Transportation Officials
444 North Capitol Street, NW, Suite 225
Washington, DC 20036

▶ International Bridge, Tunnel and Turnpike Association
2120 L Street, NW, Suite 305
Washington, DC 20037

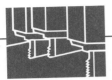

Tool and Die Makers

Other articles to look at:
► **Instrument Makers**
► **Machinists**
► **Molders**
► **Patternmakers**
► **Welders**

What tool and die makers do

Tool and die makers design and construct dies (metal forms) and other metal objects that are used in the manufacturing of many different products—such as car and airplane parts, furniture, and refrigerators and other electrical machinery. They are highly skilled workers who drill and shape metal objects so that these objects can be used in the production of both large and small items. They work in automobile, airplane, and other metalworking industries.

Tool and die makers often work from rough sketches, verbal instructions, or blueprints. They sometimes work on parts that must not vary from specifications more than one ten-millionth of an inch. To meet these strict standards, tool and die makers use precision measuring devices and hand and power tools.

After determining how a part should be made, tool and die makers measure and mark the piece of metal that will be cut to form parts of the finished product. They then use grinders and other machine and hand tools, such as files and chisels, to cut or drill the metal as specified in the instructions. All metal parts must be carefully checked to make sure they meet the specifications. Tool and die makers use measuring instruments to keep a close check on dimensions throughout the production process. After being satisfied that all parts are correctly made, tool and die makers fit the pieces together to obtain the finished product.

Tool and die makers spend most of the workday on their feet and are often required to lift or move heavy machinery. Because they work with high-speed machines, they must carefully follow safety rules and wear protective equipment—they always wear safety glasses for protection against bits of flying metal and often wear earplugs to lessen the impact of machine noise.

Education and training

Tool and die makers should have a strong interest in mechanical subjects and a superior ability to work with their hands. They should also be good at working with metal and other material and be skillful at using hand tools, power tools, and measuring devices.

Because tool and die makers often work alone or with little supervision, they must be resourceful people who start projects on their own. They should also be able to read engineering sketches and carefully follow instructions. Excellent vision is necessary, either with or without eyeglasses.

The best way to become a tool and die maker is to complete a four-year apprenticeship. During this type of program, high school graduates get on-the-job training in the use of machine tools and measuring instruments as well as classroom instruction in technical subjects such as mathematics, physics, and blueprint reading.

Some tool and die makers do not complete an apprenticeship program but rather start as machinists or machine tool operators and then become tool and die workers. Although these workers are already skilled in many of the measuring and cutting processes, they usually must be closely supervised for several months before qualifying as tool and die makers.

Earnings

Because of the increased use of automation in manufacturing processes, there will be limited opportunities for tool and die makers in the 1990s. But, because of the many years required to become trained as a tool and die maker, those skilled in this field should find good job opportunities.

The average salary is about $30,000 per year. Apprentices earn about half this amount, but their pay is increased every six months so that they are making nearly this amount by the end of their apprenticeship.

Ways of getting more information

A good way to find out about being a tool and die maker is to develop a hobby that requires patience and mechanical ability, such as model

▶ Using a small vice, a tool and die manufacturer places a piece into the machine.

making or car repair. It might also be possible to get a part-time or summer job at a machine shop and in that way learn more about the profession.

In addition, write to the following organizations and ask for information about being a tool and die maker:

▶ National Tooling and Machining Association
    9300 Livingston Road
    Fort Washington, MD 20744

▶ Tooling and Manufacturing Association
    1177 South Dee Road
    Park Ridge, IL 60068

Tour Guides

Other articles to look at:
▶ **Conductors**
▶ **Foreign-Service Officers**
▶ **Recreation Workers**
▶ **Reservation and Transportation Ticket Agents**
▶ **Travel Agents**

What tour guides do

Tour guides escort groups of travelers to different cities and countries. By acting as a link between the tourist and the area and its people, tour guides try to ensure that the trip will be as enjoyable and safe as possible.

The jobs performed by tour guides are varied. Some guides act as travel agents for the tour, booking airline flights, car rentals, and cruises. They research area hotels and other lodgings and plan sightseeing tours. Guides try to meet the needs of the group by learning individual interests. If older members of a tour, for example, did not want to climb 50 steps to visit a cathedral, the tour guide would need to plan other activities for such travelers.

Many details can be worked out before the group leaves home. Hotel reservations, special exhibits, theater tickets, and side trips can all be booked weeks or months before the tour begins. But no matter how organized a tour guide is beforehand, many problems often arise during trips, and guides must be able to act quickly and calmly to deal with them as they occur.

Guides must see that food and lodging meet expected standards and make sure all baggage and personal belongings are loaded on the plane, bus, or train and that they are handled properly. It is most important that tour guides keep track of the people on their tours. It's their responsibility to see that everyone gets home safely.

Tour guides are the sources of interesting information about the areas visited. They should be prepared to answer all kinds of questions, from details about local history to how to cash a traveler's check.

Education and training

College degrees are not necessary but are certainly helpful, especially if guides wish to lead tours to foreign countries. Courses in history, art, and foreign languages, as well as in speech and communication, are very helpful.

Some large cities have professional schools that offer classes in becoming tour guides. Community colleges may offer this training as well. Travel agencies and tour companies often provide their own training, which prepares guides to lead the tour packages they offer.

Earnings

Through the 1990s, guides will continue to be needed for conducting tours for business, recreation, and education.

▶ A tour guide explains water safety before taking a group on a river ride.

Many tour guides work only eight months, or fewer, out of the year, but they may earn up to $15,000 for those months. Many guides earn weekly salaries that average $300. Many are given tips by those on their tours. Guides receive their meals and accommodations free while conducting tours; they also receive a daily fee to cover personal expenses.

Ways of getting more information

Many large cities have zoos, theme parks, or historical districts, and giving tours in any of them provides experience on handling groups of people and giving lectures.

For more information write to the following organizations:

▶ American Society of Travel Agents
1101 King Street
Alexandria, VA 22314

▶ Travel Industry Association of America
1133 21st Street, NW
Washington, DC 20036

Toxicologists

Other articles to look at:
▶ **Biologists**
▶ **Chemists**
▶ **Pharmaceutical Technicians**
▶ **Pharmacologists**
▶ **Pollution-Control Technicians**

What toxicologists do

Toxicologists conduct research on toxic substances, which are things that are poisonous—like certain chemicals and drugs and substances that pollute rivers and lakes. They are concerned with detecting the poisons; with discovering the effects of poisons on humans, plants, and animals; and with finding treatments for poisonous conditions. Toxicology is a very large field of science, involving the disciplines of chemistry, biochemistry, pharmacology, and many others.

Toxicologists work in various different situations. For instance, a *medical toxicologist* may be part of a research team in a hospital or poison control center, where he or she might work in emergency situations to help save victims of drug overdose or accidental exposure to poisons. Medical toxicologists might also try to solve long-term issues such as the level of toxic material in cigarettes. *Industrial toxicologists* may work for a private company, such as a cosmetics firm, testing new products to determine whether certain ingredients are toxic. Workers in industrial toxicology also may be involved in identifying

toxic substances in workplaces, such as harmful gases that come from vents.

Environmental toxicologists often work for government agencies concerned with protecting consumers from accidental exposure to poisons in food and drugs. For example, they might study fish to determine the level of mercury contained in them. Their results could be used by city, state, or federal officials to limit the level of mercury that manufacturing companies use in the production process. Another area of toxicology involves identifying and working with pesticides and herbicides, which are substances designed to harm or kill insects and plants.

Toxicologists keep careful records of all their research and then write reports on their findings. They may work with legislators to write new, protective laws, or they may appear at official hearings in order to discuss policy decisions. In all their work they must be conscientious, accurate, and patient; they must keep up to date on the most modern equipment and research procedures; and, since they deal with poisonous substances, they must pay the strictest attention to safety procedures.

Education and training

Many years of training are needed to become a toxicologist. Interested persons should have a doctorate in pharmacology, chemistry, or a related science, with some post-doctorate work in toxicology as well. Today's toxicologist must also have a good working knowl edge of computers, since much of the work involves sophisticated electronic equipment. Finally, all toxicologists must be licensed, though licensing requirements vary from state to state. Most licensing procedures include a check into the applicant's education, references, and work history, as well as a comprehensive written examination.

Earnings

Employment opportunities for toxicologists are expected to grow throughout the 1990s. As our society uses more and more chemicals and other toxic substances in agriculture and industry, there will be an increased need for trained professionals to determine and limit the health risks of these toxins. Job opportunities should be greatest in cities, as this is where most large hospitals and research facilities are located. As always, those with the most training and experience will win the best jobs.

As trained medical professionals, toxicologists earn very good salaries. Those with a master's degree can expect to make $24,000 to $29,000 a year to start, while those who have earned a doctorate should make between $30,000 and $50,000 per year. Experienced toxicologists can earn as much as $80,000 a year.

Ways of getting more information

Ask your librarian for reading materials on the history and development of toxicology, or see if you can arrange a meeting with a practicing toxicologist at your local hospital or poison control center. Your science teacher can also direct you to journals and other reading material about this field.

▶ Toxicologists test chemicals to determine if the compounds are harmful.

For more information, write to the following places:

▶ American College of Toxicology
9650 Rockville Pike
Bethesda, MD 20814

▶ Society of Toxicology
1101 14th Street, NW, Suite 1100
Washington, DC 20005

Toy Industry Workers

Other articles to look at:
- ▶ **Assemblers**
- ▶ **Designers**
- ▶ **Packaging and Paper Products Technicians**
- ▶ **Plastics Products Manufacturing Workers**
- ▶ **Sporting Goods Production Workers**

What toy industry workers do

Toy industry workers put toys and games together. People in the toy industry make all kinds of products, including bicycles, video games, dolls, swing sets, puzzles, balls, and board games.

Some workers operate machines on assembly lines where each worker performs one step in making a toy. For example, some workers run machines that blow the filling into stuffed animals. Others run machines that put tires on the wheels of bicycles and tricycles. Workers may fill molds with plastic to shape the heads, arms, legs, and bodies of dolls and action figures. Other workers operate the machines that put these molded pieces together.

To make a game, some workers print the game board. Others use machines to cut out the cardboard backing and paste the game board on the backing. Some workers make only the dice for the games.

Some toy industry workers don't use machines to assemble certain toys. They may glue, cut, or nail pieces together. Or they might have to paint faces on dolls or other toys. Some workers, called *hand finishers,* dress dolls or tie ribbons around the necks of stuffed animals.

Toy industry workers work in factories. When the toys are assembled, conveyor belts carry them to other workers who use machines to wrap and package them. In a small factory, there may be one large area with about 200 workers all doing different jobs. These factories are often noisy places. Some jobs require workers to stand most of the day. In many of these jobs, workers do the same thing over and over again; still, they must keep alert to see that each toy is made properly.

From July to September, many toy companies want their workers to work ten hours a day or longer to help get toys made for the holiday season. After September, toy companies slow down, and some of them lay off their workers for part of the year. This means that some workers will have no work and no pay during the slow seasons.

Education and training

There is no special education or training for toy industry workers. They learn on-the-job skills in order to operate the machines and do hand work. Reliable workers can become supervisors who train other workers and inspect their work. To help negotiate raises and better working conditions, toy industry workers can join unions, such as the Amalgamated Toy and Novelty Workers Union.

Earnings

It is difficult to determine how good the job opportunities will be for toy industry workers. Many more toys and games are being imported from other countries, and many companies are moving their manufacturing operations out of the United States.

Many toy industry workers are paid by the hour. Most beginning workers can expect to earn the legal minimum wage, which in the 1990s is about $4.35 per hour. Experienced workers can earn $6.00 an hour or more. Workers who operate machines earn more than those who assemble toys by hand.

Some factories pay workers a certain amount for each toy they complete—this is called doing piecework. The faster they work, the more that pieceworkers can earn.

Ways of getting more information

For more information, write to the following organization:

▶ Toy Manufacturers of America
    200 Fifth Avenue, Room 740
    New York, NY 10010

▶ A toy industry worker places the mouths on toy phones.

Travel Agents

Other articles to look at:
▶ **Flight Attendants**
▶ **Hotel and Motel Management**
▶ **Reservation and Transportation Ticket Agents**
▶ **Secretaries**
▶ **Tour Guides**

What travel agents do

Travel agents help people plan vacations and business trips by providing information about transportation, hotels or motels, and sightseeing opportunities. Agents make tour reservations, prepare tickets, and advise people on passport and visa requirements. Although there is the possibility of traveling to faraway places, travel agents usually work in offices making detailed travel arrangements and then making sure those arrangements are correct.

A travel agent must be part salesperson, part travel consultant, and part bookkeeper. Agents must first discuss the travel needs of a customer (such as where and when a person wants to travel, how much money they can afford to spend, and how long they can stay away) and then present the client with a travel plan that meets those needs. The agent may suggest a package tour in one area or arrange for the person to stay in a number of places over a specified period of time.

Travel agents consult a variety of sources to get the desired arrival and departure times for planes, boats, or trains; find the most rea-

sonably priced transportation fares; and arrange hotel rooms or make other reservations. Most agents use computers to find out about flight schedules and the various prices of hotel and motel accommodations. Agents often use their own experiences when making reservations.

For inexperienced travelers, the travel agent may review what to bring on a trip and what to expect once travelers reach their destination. For example, an agent may provide travelers with a guide book and explain the best ways to change money into a foreign currency.

Agents may also give slide presentations or lectures to interested groups or place advertisements in newspapers in order to promote their services.

Education and training

Travel agents should have a well-rounded education. Good communications skills, including the ability to write and speak clearly, are important. In addition, knowledge of one or more foreign languages (Spanish, French, and so on) will be of help when dealing with travelers or other people from foreign countries. Travel agents must have a solid background in world geography and must keep up-to-date on world events so that questions about upcoming events (such as the Olympics) can be anticipated and areas experiencing conflict (such as countries having serious political problems) can be avoided. As in many other professions, computer skills are becoming increasingly important—agents are constantly using computers to make travel reservations.

Students interested in becoming travel agents should take classes in geography, English, and history, as well as business-related courses such as typing and mathematics. Many employers prefer to hire college graduates, although a person with a high school diploma may also find success. There are also special training programs for travel agents and most travel agencies give on-the-job training to new employees.

Earnings

With individuals and families continuing to take vacations and weekend trips the whole year round, job opportunities for travel agents are expected to be good during the 1990s. New job openings will occur as new agencies are started and as more agents transfer to other occupations.

Salaries for travel agents range between $12,000 and $21,000 a year, depending on experience and the size of the company. Travel agents may be paid a regular salary, they may be paid entirely on a commission basis (based on how many people use their services), or they may receive a salary plus a commission. An advantage of working as a travel agent is that when agents themselves take a trip, they get substantially reduced prices on airplane tickets and hotel rates. Sometimes, an agent may get a free (or almost free) trip for promotional purposes.

Ways of getting more information

A good way to find out about being a travel agent is to visit a travel agency and talk to the people who work there. Reading about people who travel and about their experiences is also a good way to learn more about this career.

▶ A travel agent explains train schedules to a couple planning a trip abroad.

In addition, write to the following and ask for information about being a travel agent:

▶ American Society of Travel Agents
   1101 King Street
   Alexandria, VA 22314

▶ Institute of Certified Travel Agents
   148 Linden Street
   Wellesley, MA 02181

▶ American Guides Association
   8909 Dorrington Avenue
   West Hollywood, CA 90048

Truck and Delivery Drivers

Other articles to look at:
- ► **Collection Workers**
- ► **Industrial-Truck Operators**
- ► **Manufacturers' Sales Representatives**
- ► **Public Transportation Operators**

What truck and delivery drivers do

Truck and delivery drivers operate trucks and vans over long and short distances and make deliveries from producers to customers. *Long haulers,* also known as *trailer-truck drivers,* transport goods over long distances in gasoline- or diesel-powered tractor-trailers. They often drive from state to state and might go as far as across the country, frequently driving at night. Long haulers must be highly skilled at their work. They must be able to back up their huge trailers to loading docks and inspect their trucks before and after long trips and keep a daily log.

Two types of employers hire long haulers: private and for-hire carriers. Private carriers include chain food stores and large manufacturing plants that pick up and deliver their own goods. For-hire carriers are trucking firms that serve both the general public (common carriers) and specific companies (contract carriers). Drivers who work for common and contract carriers often own or lease their own trucks.

Short haulers, also known as *local truck drivers* and *delivery drivers,* operate vehicles to deliver merchandise within a limited area. These local drivers often drive small trucks or vans within specified neighborhoods delivering such goods as bread, soft drinks, and ice cream to stores. They often collect the payment from the stores they deliver to, and some also must try to get new customers for their products.

Local drivers may be expected to make minor repairs to their vehicles and otherwise keep them in good working order. They also must be very skilled drivers because they have to maneuver their trucks through congested city traffic, fit their vehicles into tight parking spaces, and sometimes drive through narrow alleys. These drivers usually load and unload their own vehicles.

Local drivers of heavy trucks (over three tons) generally have a helper who assists with the loading and unloading of the truck. Drivers of moving vans usually have a crew of helpers. Some heavy-truck drivers operate special vehicles, including dump trucks, oil and gasoline trucks, and cement-mixing trucks.

Education and training

A high school education is desirable for persons wanting to become truck drivers. All workers must have a driver's license from the state in which they live, and of course employers want workers with good driving records. Drivers' education courses and auto shop classes are especially helpful for those who do not yet know how to drive.

▶ Using a citizen's band radio, a truck driver radios to other drivers to find out about road and traffic conditions.

Most employers of delivery drivers provide on-the-job training during which the new driver will work a delivery route with an experienced driver. Most trucking companies prefer to hire drivers who are at least between 21 and 25 years old. Employees must pass certain physical exams that check vision, use of arms and legs, and blood pressure. Often drivers must be able to lift heavy objects. Long haulers must meet standards set by the U.S. Department of Transportation.

Earnings

Local drivers are usually paid by the hour, and long haulers are generally paid by the mile. Average hourly earnings for all drivers is about $11.60. Those working for trucking companies usually earn the highest wages, as much as $50,000 per year.

Ways of getting more information

For more information write to:

▶   American Trucking Associations
    2200 Mill Road
    Alexandria, VA 22314

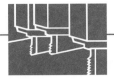

Typesetters

Other articles to look at:
▶ **Bindery Workers**
▶ **Lithographic Workers**
▶ **Photoengravers**
▶ **Printing Press Operators**
▶ **Typists**

What typesetters do

Anything that is printed in mass form must first pass through the hands of the typesetter before it goes on to the printing press. *Typesetters* enter words into computers that are programmed to do such things as hyphenate words and create columns of text. This task is called keyboarding. Typesetters prepare the type for all kinds of printed matter: newspapers, books, magazines, advertisements, business forms, and so on.

Typesetters first select the type style and size according to instructions for the job to be done. They then arrange, or set, the type in correct order and in the proper place on the page, along with any necessary breaks or photoengravings (photos). Type can be set by hand or on the keyboard of a linotype or monotype machine, but most typesetters today use the electronic keyboard of a computerized phototypesetting machine.

After the type has been properly set, a sample of the printed material is made. This sample, called a proof, is carefully examined for mistakes so that the typesetter can correct them before final copies are printed.

Typesetters must be careful, accurate workers with a thorough understanding of the mechanical or electronic machines they use. They need a good command of the English language and should be proficient in spelling, grammar, and arithmetic.

Education and training

A high school education is usually a requirement for becoming a typesetter, with courses in printing and typing being especially good preparation. Most typesetters learn their trade as helpers or apprentices on the job. Apprenticeships usually take from four to six years, depending on the individual's previous experience and education. Helpers, who usually work in small nonunion shops, pick up their skills in the course of their work.

Graphic arts programs at community and junior colleges often have courses about the printing industry. Printing courses are also offered at many vocational schools.

There are many different occupations in the printing field, so advancement opportunities are plentiful for ambitious workers. One common ambition of typesetters and printers is to have shops of their own, and many of the printing establishments in this country are one-person shops operated by their owners.

Earnings

Job opportunities for typesetters in the 1990s will be average, even though the printing in-

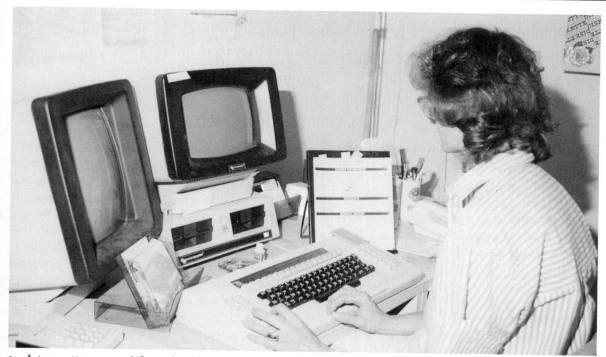

▶ A typesetter enters information into the computer with printing codes to set type size and style.

dustry is expected to grow. New computer technology has made typesetting tasks easier and quicker to perform, so fewer employees are thus needed. Furthermore, more and more companies are doing printing tasks such as typesetting within their own firms, with improved computer desktop publishing programs. It will be the workers with the greatest technical knowledge and abilities who find the best jobs in the future.

The average yearly salary for typesetters is about $17,000. Some experienced workers who have been in the business for many years, however, make as much as $30,000 per year.

industry. For a firsthand look at what typesetters do, try to arrange a visit to a newspaper or other commercial printing establishment.

For more information write to:

▶ Book Manufacturers Institute
111 Prospect
Stamford, CT 06901

▶ Printing Industries of America
100 Daingerfield Road
Alexandria, VA 22314

▶ Typographers International Association
2233 Wisconsin, Suite 235
Washington, DC 20007

Ways of getting more information
Libraries have many books and magazines on the history and development of the printing

129

Typists

What typists do

Typewriters, word-processing machines, and other office equipment are important parts of any work place. *Typists* use these machines to change handwritten material into clean, easy-to-read typewritten copies. They work on reports, letters, forms, charts, and many other projects for all types of businesses and services. Word-processing machines are computers that are used to store material electronically instead of printing it directly on paper. These machines are quickly replacing typewriters in many offices, even though both are still in wide use.

For some typists, their only duty is to type. Others spend much of their time typing but also have clerical jobs such as filing, answering the phone, and running the copy machine. A worker may be the only typist in a small office, or he or she may be part of a group of typists (called a typing pool), with as many as a hundred or more. Most typists work in modern, well-lighted, pleasant surroundings.

Among the different types of workers in this field are *clerk typists,* who type reports, bills, and forms; *data entry keyers,* who type mostly numerical data from checks, bills, and invoices into computer systems; and *word processors,* who operate word-processing machines. The keyboard of a word-processor is much like that of a typewriter except that the numbers and letters show up on a video display terminal (VDT). These typists can edit, change, and insert material just by pressing keys, which make the changes on the machine. When word-processing operators have finished typing a document, it is automatically sent to a dot-matrix or laser printer, which produces a document that looks typewritten.

Education and training

Most typists should have a high school diploma and be able to type neatly, correctly, and quickly. Typists should have a good knowledge of spelling, grammar, and punctuation. The skills needed for the typist are taught in high schools, colleges, business schools, and home-study courses. In addition, computer and word-processing classes are taught at most community colleges and business schools.

For those who have not had word-processing training in school, many employers provide training to new employees. The makers of word-processing equipment also offer classes to introduce the basics of operating their equipment. In general, it takes three to six months of hands-on experience to become a good word-processing operator.

▶ With the information to be typed on a board beside her, a typist copies the information onto another page.

Earnings

More than one million people were employed as typists, word processors, and data entry keyers during the 1990s. Most worked in business, but many others worked in education, medicine, and government. The demand for typists, however, is expected to decline mainly because of the increasing use of automated office equipment, which makes tasks easier and quicker to perform.

The average yearly pay for typists in large city areas is about $14,612, while data entry keyers earn about $15,002 and word processors average approximately $18,148.

Ways of getting more information

A good way to get experience in this field is through a high school work/study program. Students in these programs work part-time for local businesses and go to school part-time.

For additional information write to the following:

▶ Professional Secretaries International
   10502 Northwest Ambassador Drive
   Kansas City, MO 64195

Umpires

Other articles to look at:
► **Athletes**
► **Judges**
► **Recreation Workers**
► **Sports Coaches**

What umpires do

Umpires and other sports officials enforce the rules and regulations of a particular sport and make decisions on disputed matters during sporting contests. The term *umpire* is usually used to refer to those who officiate at baseball games; those who officiate at basketball, football, soccer, and other sports games are often called *referees* or *linesmen*. Although umpires regulate professional baseball games, the vast majority work for minor league and amateur teams.

An umpire must often start work well before a game begins. Umpires inspect the playing field before the game to make sure it is in good condition and check the baseballs and bats to see that they are regulation size and weight.

During the game, umpires must carefully watch the action. There are usually four umpires at a professional baseball game; amateur contests may have one or two umpires. Each umpire has specific responsibilities. For example, the *plate umpire* calls balls and strikes. This requires careful attention and quick decisions after the pitcher throws the ball. When the ball is hit, the umpires watch it to see if it lands in fair or foul territory and to see if a fielder catches the ball or if it falls safely into play. Umpires must be careful not to interfere with play and not to make decisions too quickly because an outfielder may drop a ball at the last second or a fielder may illegally block a player from running around the bases.

Sometimes umpires must make important decisions that anger and upset some of the players and fans. Umpires may get into arguments with managers and players, but more often than not, umpires make their decisions without much controversy.

Umpires must travel a great deal. Professional umpires travel around the country and rarely spend more than a day or two at home during the season. Amateur umpires work closer to home, but they also travel a great deal and work evenings and weekends.

Education and training

Umpires and other sports officials should have a comprehensive understanding of a sport and its rules. They also need good judgment, integrity, and the ability to make quick, accurate decisions. Umpires should also have excellent eyesight (with or without correction) and be in good physical condition.

Umpires may be called on to make important decisions in a matter of seconds. They must have confidence in their ability to make such decisions and should be able to handle the pressure of having people disagree with them (sometimes rather strongly).

There are no specific educational requirements. Umpires at the amateur level are often former players or coaches who understand the game and know the rules. These umpires may attend a one-day clinic several times a year to review the rules and discuss umpiring techniques. Those who want to umpire on the professional level should have at least several years of minor league umpiring experience and complete a two-month training program at a school for umpires. These programs feature a comprehensive review of the rules and regulations. Many of the classes are taught by professional umpires.

Earnings

There are only limited opportunities to work as umpires, especially at the professional level. There are fewer than 100 major league umpires, and minor league opportunities are also fairly rare.

Earnings vary greatly, depending on which level an umpire is employed at. Major league umpires earn about $75,000 per year, with bonuses for working championship games such as the World Series. Minor league umpires earn about $1,200 a month, but they normally work only during the summer months. Other umpires may earn $15 to $20 per game.

Ways of getting more information

A good way to find out if you would enjoy being an umpire is to officiate at a summer

▶ An umpire watches a race to the plate to determine if the runner made it there first.

camp or work for a Little League or similar organization. It might also be possible to talk with an umpire and in that way learn more about the profession.

In addition, write to the following organizations and ask for information about being an umpire:

▶ Major League Umpires Association
  1 Logan Square, Suite 1004
  Philadelphia, PA 19103

▶ National Association of Leagues, Umpires and Scorers
  PO Box 1420
  Wichita, KS 67201

Underwriters

Other articles to look at:
▶ **Actuaries**
▶ **Bank Services Occupations**
▶ **Insurance Claims Representatives**
▶ **Insurance Policy Processing Occupations**
▶ **Life Insurance Agents and Brokers**

What underwriters do

Underwriters decide whether an insurance company should agree to insure someone and how much that person will have to pay for insurance.

People want insurance to protect themselves against serious accidents or big losses. For example, if a family's house burns down, they may not be able to afford to buy another one. To protect themselves in case this happens, they apply for fire insurance. This means that the family pays the insurance company a certain amount of money, perhaps once a month or once per year. Then if the house does burn down, the insurance company pays the family an amount of money to help them buy a new one. In other words, the insurance company will cover the risk of fire for that family.

The insurance company can afford to cover one family's loss because it receives money every month from many families who do not lose their houses. Insurance companies have to make sure that they do not cover risks that would be financially unsound. It is the underwriter's job to make sure that the insurance company does not take bad risks. For example, if someone wants fire insurance on a building with bad wiring or an unsafe furnace, the underwriter may decide that the risk of fire in this building is too great. Then the underwriter can either refuse to insure the building; agree to insure it after repairs are made; or charge a higher monthly payment for insurance.

Underwriters work in offices, receiving applications from people who want insurance for all kinds of things. Life insurance will pay a specified person if the insured person dies; disability insurance will pay insured workers who have accidents or illnesses that prevent them from working; property insurance covers damage or loss of almost any kind of property—houses, boats, jewelry, cars, bridges, airplanes, paintings, and so on.

Underwriters must look at the information in each application carefully. They have to analyze what kinds of risks are involved. Then they study statistics on how likely these risks are to occur. Underwriters make decisions based on many technical details. They must be able to weigh all the facts and take responsibility for their decisions. Insurance companies depend on the good judgment of their underwriters.

Education and training

Most insurance companies look for college graduates to fill underwriting jobs. The bach-

▶ An underwriter prepares a report on the insurance policy of a prospective client.

elor's degree may be in any field, although a degree in business may be especially helpful. Most insurance companies want their underwriters to keep up with new developments in the field by taking part-time classes.

Earnings

As the insurance business expands in the 1990s, job opportunities for underwriters are expected to be good. Average yearly salaries depend on whether one works for individual insurance or for business insurance and also on how much experience one has. A beginning underwriter might earn about $23,400 per year; supervisors in business insurance earn about $40,000; and some managers earn up to $49,000 per year.

Ways of getting more information

Talking with an insurance agent will give you an idea of how insurance companies work and what different jobs are available.

For more information write to:

▶ American Council of Life Insurance
   1001 Pennsylvania Avenue, NW
   Washington, DC 20004

▶ Insurance Information Institute
   110 William Street
   New York, NY 10038

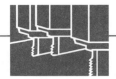

Vending-Machine Mechanics

Other articles to look at:
- ▶ **Appliance Repairers**
- ▶ **Electromechanical Technicians**
- ▶ **Industrial Machinery Mechanics**
- ▶ **Machinists**
- ▶ **Office-Machine Servicers**

What vending-machine mechanics do

Vending machines, which are coin-operated machines that dispense items such as soft drinks, soup, sandwiches, and candy, can be found in stores, schools, and many other locations. *Vending-machine mechanics* install these machines and keep them in good operating condition. They test new machines to make sure they are working properly, check and clean them on a regular basis, and make any necessary repairs.

Before new machines are installed, mechanics make sure they are in good working order. Most vending machines have complicated electrical connections that require close inspection. A beverage dispenser, for example, has ice-making and refrigerator systems for cold drinks or heating units for coffee and other hot drinks. Mechanics must make sure that the machine mixes the drinks properly, that the dispenser does not overfill or underfill the cups, and that the change-making system works. When installing the machines, mechanics connect the machines to electrical and water sources. Then they fill the machines with ingredients or products and retest them for proper operations.

When a machine breaks down, mechanics must figure out the cause of the problem. Loose electrical wires, coin-operation troubles, and beverage leaks are relatively easy to spot; more difficult problems might require the use of a testing device to find defective parts. Mechanics often repair or replace broken parts at the site, but for complicated problems they might replace the machine and bring the broken one to the repair shop.

A major part of the mechanics' job is preventative maintenance. They check the machines regularly to prevent problems before they occur. For example, they put grease on mechanical parts and clean electrical connections to keep the machines performing properly. This is especially important with machines that are used a great deal (as many of them are).

Mechanics also have some clerical responsibilities, such as writing reports, preparing cost estimates, and ordering parts. They also stock the machines with merchandise, collect the money, make sure the machines have enough coins to make change, and keep daily sales records.

Education and training

Vending-machine mechanics should have an interest in electronics and mechanical things and be able to work with their hands. They need to be skillful in using hammers, screwdrivers, and other hand tools and power tools. Because mechanics handle certain amounts of cash, they should be trustworthy.

A pleasant personality is important so that mechanics can deal effectively with the many different types of people in the businesses and other locations where the machines are located.

Most mechanics learn their skills on the job by working alongside experienced mechanics for several weeks or months. New workers usually start by doing simple tasks such as putting products into a machine, and gradually learn how to repair and replace broken equipment. Although most employers prefer to hire high school graduates, a degree is not always necessary.

A three-year apprenticeship program is offered by the National Automatic Merchandising Association to help employers train workers. The program provides several weeks of classroom training each year in subjects such as basic electronics, blueprint reading, customer relations, and safety.

▶ With the cup dispenser pulled out, a vending-machine mechanic refills the supplies in the machine.

Earnings

Although more and more establishments are installing vending machines, future job opportunities will be somewhat limited. This is because newer machines break down less often and therefore require less maintenance. Despite limited job opportunities, skilled mechanics should continue to find employment.

Vending-machine mechanics usually get paid an hourly rate. The average pay is between $7.00 and $14.00 per hour.

Ways of getting more information

To find out more about vending-machine mechanics, take a course in machine repair or get a part-time job as a mechanic's helper.

In addition, write to the following organization and ask for information about being a vending-machine mechanic:

▶ National Automatic Merchandising Association
  20 North Wacker Drive
  Chicago, IL 60606

▶ National Bulk Vendors Association
  200 North LaSalle Street, Room 2100
  Chicago, IL 60601

Veterinarians

Other articles to look at:
► **Agricultural Engineers**
► **Animal Health Technicians**
► **Veterinary Technicians**
► **Zoo and Aquarium Curators and Directors**
► **Zoologists**

What veterinarians do

Veterinarians are doctors who treat diseased and injured animals and give advice on how to care for and breed healthy animals. Veterinarians treat not only dogs, cats, and other small pets, but may also work with farm and zoo animals. Still others do research to find causes and cures of diseases.

Most veterinarians work with small animals that people have as companions, such as dogs, cats, and birds. They do surgery, treat minor illnesses, and board animals, both sick and healthy ones, who need a temporary place to stay. Sometimes they provide emergency house calls, but most try to keep normal business hours. A number of doctors may work as many as 60 hours a week if emergency health problems occur.

Other veterinarians work with larger animals or may even work with both large animals and small house pets. These doctors may specialize in the treatment and care of animals such as horses, cattle, and sheep. Others specialize in treating fish or poultry, such as ducks and geese.

In small towns or in the country, veterinarians may travel long distances to treat animals. Some large cattle ranches or horse farms keep veterinarians on their staff. Most zoos also employ a full-time veterinarian to handle the health care, feeding, and treatment of the entire animal population.

Many veterinarians work as inspectors in the food industry, such as in meat packing and chicken processing companies. They examine the meat for signs of disease. A small number of veterinarians also teach in schools of veterinary medicine.

Education and training

To set up private practice as a veterinarian, a person must have a degree as a doctor of veterinary medicine (D.V.M.) and pass an examination by a state licensing board. Usually a degree can be achieved seven or eight years after graduation from high school. Most accredited schools of veterinary medicine in the United States offer four-year programs, but some require five years to complete the degree. And most require that a student complete at least two years of general college courses before being admitted to the veterinarian program. Upon completion of a D.V.M. degree, students are required to pass an examination from the state board of licensing.

Many preveterinary students obtain a bachelor's degree from a four-year college before applying for admission to the D.V.M. degree program. Because of limited facilities, less than half of the students applying to schools of veterinary medicine are admitted. Good grades in high school and preveterinary college are essential.

Earnings

The job outlook for vets in the 1990s is expected to be good. There will probably always be a demand for veterinarians, although competition for jobs may be stiff. Those with the best training will have the most opportunity for advancement.

Generally, veterinarians just starting out in private practice can expect to make about $23,000 per year. Those in more established careers can make between $40,000 and $60,000 per year. Those who work for the federal government will make slightly less.

Ways of getting more information

Visiting with local veterinarians in their office, at a farm, a ranch, a zoo, or at a college or a university is an excellent way to learn more about the day-to-day work of veterinarians.

In school, study biology and animal-related sciences. Joining a 4-H Club and participating in projects involving the care of animals is also valuable. Many veterinarians accept volunteers to help with feeding the animals and cleaning their cages. Part-time or summer work may also be available in veterinary offices, in zoos, or on farms.

For more information write to the following sources:

▶ American Veterinary Medical Association
    930 North Meacham Road
    Schaumburg, IL 60196

▶ Canadian Veterinary Medical Association
    339 Booth Street
    Ottawa, Ontario, Canada K1R 7KI

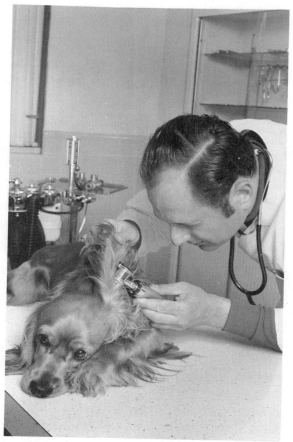

▶ A veterianarian examines a sick dog's ear.

▶ American Association of Zoo
   Veterinarians
    3400 Grand Avenue
    Philadelphia, PA 19104

Veterinary Technicians

Other articles to look at:
▶ **Animal Health Technicians**
▶ **Equestrian Management**
▶ **Fish-Production Technicians**
▶ **Veterinarians**
▶ **Zookeepers**

What veterinary technicians do

Veterinary technicians are professionals who assist veterinarians in caring for animals. They have received medical training similar to that of nurses and technicians who assist doctors.

Veterinary technicians are qualified to perform medical procedures such as taking temperatures, checking for diseases or parasites, and administering medicines. They dress wounds, clean teeth, take X rays, and treat injuries.

Technicians work closely with veterinarians during examinations and surgery. They set up machinery, sterilize instruments, and administer anesthetic to the patient. Often they also prepare an animal for surgery and care for it after the operation.

Some veterinary technicians are responsible for a hospital's pharmacy, and they dispense medicine, drugs, and vaccines. Many perform laboratory work, like taking and analyzing blood or urine.

Veterinary technicians must enjoy working with animals, and be able to handle them when they are sick, distraught, or violent.

They also must be sympathetic with pet owners, and able to follow the veterinarian's instructions.

In smaller clinics, veterinary technicians may have a variety of administrative duties, like answering the phone, maintaining records, and recording animal histories. Those in larger clinics may have specific tasks such as caring for one type of animal. In addition, exotic pets, like snakes, birds, and lizards, are very popular, and some veterinarian clinics need trained staff members who specialize in care of exotic animals.

Most veterinary technicians work in animal clinics and hospitals. Those working in rural areas with domestic animals such as horses, cows, and sheep are called animal health technicians. Others help conduct research that uses animals in laboratories and pharmaceutical companies. There are many different industries where animals are found and all need veterinary technicians. Breeding kennels and zoos are just a few examples.

Education and training

Veterinary technicians must graduate from a two-year program that is accredited by the American Veterinary Medical Association. Some four-year programs lead to a bachelor's degree. Courses include chemistry, mathematics, animal husbandry, veterinary anatomy, surgical assisting, pharmacology, and radiography. Students also receive practical training working with live animals.

To enter these programs, a student must have a high school diploma. Other requirements vary by program. Interested high school students should prepare by taking science courses, as well as classes in English, chemistry, algebra, and physics. Experience in working with animals also is an advantage.

Earnings

There will be an increased demand for trained veterinary technicians in the 1990s. Pet ownership is growing, and more animal hospitals and clinics are hiring qualified staff.

Wages for veterinary technicians vary, depending on the level of experience and education of the technician and on the size and geographic location of the employer. Beginning salaries average from $11,700 to $19,000 a year. Those with more experience can earn from $16,000 to $27,000 a year.

▶ A veterinary technician works closely with a veterinarian to keep a cat quiet while listening to its heartbeat.

Ways of getting more information

A good way to find out if you would enjoy working with animals is to volunteer time or take a part-time job at an animal shelter or zoo. Also, you can call a local animal clinic or shelter to arrange an interview with the veterinary technicians to inquire about the rewards and responsibilities of this field.

In addition, write to:

▶ American Veterinary Medical Association
    930 North Meacham Road
    Schaumburg, IL 60196

▶ American Association of Zoo Veterinarians
    3400 Girard Avenue
    Philadelphia, PA 19104

▶ Canadian Veterinary Medical Association
    339 Booth Street
    Ottawa, Ontario, Canada K1R 7K1

Video Technicians

Other articles to look at:
- ▶ **Audio-Control Technicians**
- ▶ **Communications Equipment Mechanics**
- ▶ **Radio and Television Program Directors**
- ▶ **Sound-Recording Technicians**
- ▶ **Studio Technicians**

What video technicians do

Video technicians usually work in television stations. They can also work with video production houses on business, advertising, and documentary productions. They are involved in several different aspects of broadcasting and videotaping television programs. Technicians who are mostly involved with broadcasting programs are often called *video-control technicians*. Those who are mostly involved with taping programs are often called *videotape-recording technicians*.

Video-control technicians work under the direction of the television program director. They operate equipment that controls the picture that is sent to the transmitter for broadcast. During a studio production, several cameras record the show, and the picture from each camera is displayed in the studio control room. The director indicates which camera's picture should be used, and the technician switches that picture to the transmitter or videotape machine. Video-control technicians also control the quality of the picture by op-erating switches that adjust color balance, brightness, framing, vertical hold, and contrast.

Some programs require that video-control technicians combine pictures coming from different sources. They may mix together scenes being performed in different studios, blend live segments with taped ones, or switch between studio and on-the-scene transmissions. The broadcasting of instant replays, which are very common in live sports events, is another responsibility of video-control technicians.

In addition, video-control technicians monitor programs that are on the air to make sure that their picture quality is good. They also keep a daily record of all programs that are sent to the transmitter.

Videotape-recording technicians use special cameras and tape-recording equipment to videotape live shows. They also copy segments from one videotape to another in order to combine several scenes into a finished program. They sometimes create special effects using the recording and rerecording equipment.

Videotape-recording technicians prepare for a show by checking that their equipment is in working order and by making sure that they understand what they are to record and how they are to record it. During the show they monitor sound and picture quality and make adjustments as necessary.

Videotape-recording technicians also do routine maintenance on their equipment and sometimes do minor repairs.

Education and training

While in high school, students interested in this career should take courses in mathematics, science (especially courses that include physics), and English. They should also try to take radio and television broadcasting or electronics courses.

After high school, they need to receive further training in television technology at a technical institute or a junior or community college that offers a two-year course of study in television broadcasting and electronics.

Earnings

The number of people employed as video technicians is expected to increase in the 1990s. However, there will be strong competition for jobs in big cities, where the number of applicants will probably exceed the number of jobs available. Opportunities may be much better in small cities, although earnings there may be lower.

Video technicians earn salaries that average about $22,000 per year. Beginning technicians usually earn less than this amount, but very experienced technicians can earn as much as $50,000 a year or more. Technicians working in cities make more than those in rural areas. Those who work for educational television stations usually earn less than those who work for commercial stations.

Ways of getting more information

A good way to learn more about this career is through a visit to a local television station. Students can also explore this field by belonging to a high school club or other organization that is involved with electronics or radio and television broadcasting.

▶ A video technician cuts and edits videotape on a splicing machine.

In addition, students can write for more information to the following organizations:

▶ National Association Broadcast Employees and Technicians
7101 Wisconsin Avenue, Suite 800
Bethesda, MD 20814

▶ National Association of Broadcasters
1771 N Street, NW
Washington, DC 20036

143

Waiters and Waitresses

Other articles to look at:
- ► **Bartenders**
- ► **Cooks and Chefs**
- ► **Flight Attendants**
- ► **Food Service Workers**
- ► **Restaurant Managers**

What waiters and waitresses do

Waiters and waitresses are part of the food service industry. Their primary function is to serve food and beverages to customers in restaurants and other food establishments. In addition to this task, waiters and waitresses also take customers' orders, make out bills, and collect money.

Many waiters and waitresses work in small, casual food establishments. These include diners, fast-food restaurants, grills, cafeterias, and sandwich shops. In addition to their regular duties, they may also be required to clear and clean tables and counters. As part of servicing their customers, they may prepare salads and beverages, dish out prepared foods such as soups and stews, replenish supplies, and set up tables for future customers. In some establishments, waiters and waitresses are also expected to clean equipment, sweep and mop floors, and carry out trash.

Many fancier, formal restaurants employ waiters and waitresses to perform specific tasks. For example, there is often a *headwaiter* or *headwaitress* who greets arriving customers, checks on their reservations, and escorts them to their tables. These employees are sometimes called *captains*. The waiter or waitress who takes the diners' orders may make suggestions about which dishes are especially appetizing. They may also recite a list of specials—dishes that the chef has prepared especially for that evening and that do not appear on the menu.

Some waiters and waitresses specialize in dispensing alcoholic and nonalcoholic beverages. These employees are called *bartenders*. Many formal restaurants also employ waiters and waitresses whose sole responsibility is to serve wine. These *wine stewards* present a list of available wines to the diners and may make suggestions about which wines would be appropriate with the food the diners have ordered. The wine steward then brings the diner's selection to the table, opens the bottle, and pours the wine. Periodically throughout the meal, the wine steward will return to refill the diners' glasses.

Waiters and waitresses do not work in restaurants only. Some work in bars, in hotel dining rooms, and in the dining cars of trains. In large hotels, room service waiters and waitresses bring food from the hotel's kitchen to the rooms of the hotel guests.

Education and training

Although there are no formal educational requirements to become waiters and waitresses, persons interested in such a career are advised to earn a high school diploma.

▶ A waitress takes a family's order for dinner and then brings the food to the table.

Most restaurants like to train their own waiters and waitresses.

Many vocational schools offer training programs for waiters and waitresses along with full programs in food service management.

Earnings

Job opportunities for waiters and waitresses are expected to be very good during the 1990s. Many workers each year are needed to fill positions left open by those leaving their jobs to pursue other types of employment.

Most waiters and waitresses earn a combination of hourly wages and customer tips. In the 1990s waiters and waitresses earned an average of $4.70 per hour, including tips. Some earned as much as $9.00.

Ways of getting more information

For more information write to:

▶ Educational Foundation of the National Restaurant Association
250 South Wacker Drive
Chicago, IL 60606

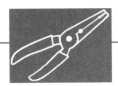

Watch and Clock Repairers

Other articles to look at:
- ▶ **Assemblers**
- ▶ **Instrument Repairers**
- ▶ **Jewelers**
- ▶ **Locksmiths**
- ▶ **Mechanical Technicians**

What watch and clock repairers do

Watch and clock repairers repair, adjust, clean, and regulate watches, clocks, and other kinds of timepieces. They may work at home or in department stores, shopping centers, jewelry stores, or repair shops.

Watches and clocks are complex machines with many small parts, and to repair them requires precision and delicacy. The first skill a repairer needs is the ability to determine exactly what is wrong with the timepiece. Asking the customer about the history of the item and current problem gives some information; visually observing and checking the winding stem may give other clues. The next step is to open the case and remove the dial so the mechanism itself can be examined using a loupe, which is a small magnifying glass.

Watch and clock repairers check for such defects as broken parts, rusting springs, and misalignment of parts. They clean, oil, repair, replace, and rebuild parts as necessary before reassembling the piece so that everything fits together properly. They use a variety of tools to help them, from simple pliers and tweezers to sophisticated electronic timing devices.

Everything they do requires great patience and a delicate touch, and experienced and skilled repairers are always in demand.

Some repairers also do jewelry repair work and sell items like those that they fix, in addition to china and silverware. This is especially true if they are self-employed or work in a retail store.

Education and training

The best way to become a watch or clock repairer is to complete the training offered by an established repair school. This training takes one to three years to complete, and the course of study includes taking apart and putting together watches, cleaning and oiling the working mechanisms, and repairing and replacing parts in various kinds of timepieces. Those persons interested in going into business for themselves would also benefit from basic business, advertising, and accounting courses, and from training in engraving, jewelry repair, and stone setting.

Although a high school diploma is not necessarily required to become a successful watch repairer, those with a diploma will find greater ease in advancement and in business dealings.

Earnings

Though skilled watch and clock repairers will always be in demand, general job opportunities in this field will be below average through

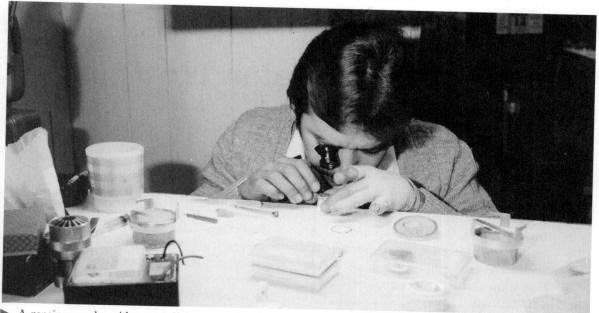

▶ A repairer works with a magnifying glass that fits against his eye when fixing the tiny pieces in a watch.

the next decade. People continue to buy inexpensive watches and clocks; it is often cheaper and easier to replace broken ones than it is to fix them. However, the person who owns a good watch will usually continue to have it repaired, and ambitious workers can endeavor to open their own repair shops or retail watch and jewelry stores.

In the 1990s, beginning watch and clock repairers earned anywhere from $9,100 to $14,600 a year. Experienced workers earned from $15,600 to more than $26,000, and supervisors and service managers in large repair shops earned considerably more. Self-employed watchmakers earned between $15,000 and $23,000 a year, while those who sold jewelry, china, and other items in addition to watches could earn up to $40,000 a year, or even more.

Ways of getting more information

Libraries have books on the subject of watchmaking and repairing; for a closer look, visit a local watchmaker and observe him or her at work. Any hobbies that call for careful handwork could serve as useful preparation as well.

For more information write to:

▶ American Watchmakers Institute
3700 Harrison Avenue
Cincinnati, OH 45211

▶ Jewelers of America
1271 Avenue of the Americas
New York, NY 10020

Water and Wastewater Treatment-Plant Operators

Other articles to look at:
▶ **Chemical Technicians**
▶ **Civil Engineering Technicians**
▶ **Health and Regulatory Inspectors**
▶ **Industrial Machinery Mechanics**
▶ **Pollution-Control Technicians**

What water and wastewater treatment-plant operators do

Water and wastewater treatment-plant operators run the plants that take harmful chemicals and wastes out of water. They make sure the water is safe to use again. They are also called *sewage plant operators.*

Water treatment plants receive water that is pumped from wells, rivers, and streams; wastewater treatment plants receive the waste materials that are carried by water through sewer pipes from all communities. Water that flows to these plants contains solid materials or microorganisms that could spread disease. It also contains industrial waste— chemicals, such as mercury and lead—that are poisonous. At the treatment plant, this wastewater, or sewage, goes through different cleaning processes until all the dangerous materials are removed.

Plant operators control the flow of water into the plant. During floods, they have to make emergency adjustments. As the sewage flows from one processing pool to another, the plant operators make sure all the equipment is working properly. If necessary, they make minor repairs.

Operators take samples of the wastewater at different stages to check its waste content. They also perform laboratory tests on the waste and keep a record of plant operations. Increasingly, operators are using computers to help them monitor their procedures. Specialized software is available that allows them to store information on the water samples they collect.

Because clean water is absolutely necessary for any community, the federal government requires that the water coming from treatment plants meet standards of cleanliness. As government standards become stricter, the process of treating wastewater becomes more complicated. Plant operators must be able to understand different processes and operate complicated machinery. Depending on the source of water for a community, the operation may need to filter out salt from sea water, chemicals from fresh water, and minerals from mountain water. Each source has different requirements.

Wastewater treatment plants must keep running night and day, so the operators work in shifts around the clock. During emergencies, they may have to work extra hours. Operators work both indoors and outdoors, checking and repairing equipment.

Most operators are employed by local governments; some work for the federal government or utility companies. In larger treatment plants, the operator will supervise attendants who perform routine tasks. In small plants, one operator may be responsible for running the entire plant.

Education and training

Most employers prefer to hire high school graduates for plant operator jobs, especially since computers are being used more and more. High school courses in mathematics and machine shop will be useful. Beyond high school, there are two-year programs in wastewater technology; however, beginning sewage plant operators often learn their skills on the job. They begin as trainees and work with an experienced operator.

Some plants may offer training programs. State water pollution control agencies offer courses to keep operators up-to-date and to expand their knowledge of water treatment processes.

In large cities, the operator jobs may require applicants to take a civil service exam. In most states, an operator who supervises a plant must be certified. To earn certification, operators must pass an exam.

Earnings

The demand for wastewater treatment-plant operators will grow only slightly in the 1990s. However, these workers usually have steady jobs because the service they provide is always essential.

Salaries vary depending on how large the plant is and the difficulty of the operator's job. The average yearly salary for a sewage plant operator is about $21,300. Supervisors earn an average of $27,200 per year.

▶ Dipping a sample collector into the treatment tank, a water treatment-plant operator checks the quality of the water.

Ways of getting more information

Making a field trip to a local water and wastewater treatment plant would be a good way to learn about this job.

For further information write to the following addresses:

▶ Nat'l. Environmental Training Assoc.
8687 Via De Ventura, Suite 214
Scottsdale, AZ 85258

▶ Water Pollution Control Federation
601 Wythe Street
Alexandria, VA 22314

Welders

Other articles to look at:
- ▶ **Aircraft Mechanics**
- ▶ **Automobile-Body Repairers**
- ▶ **Automobile Mechanics**
- ▶ **Forge Shop Workers**
- ▶ **Sheet-Metal Workers**

What welders do

The ancient art of welding, which involves the task of joining two pieces of metal together, has long since adapted the most modern technology for its uses. *Welders* join metal pieces together by applying heat, pressure, or both, until the edges of the metals meet and the pieces are permanently fused. This process is used in the manufacturing and repair of thousands of different products, from water faucets and refrigerators to cars, airplanes, and missiles.

There are more than 40 different welding processes. These procedures can be grouped into three categories: arc welding, gas welding, and resistance welding. In arc welding the worker strikes an arc (that is, he or she creates an electric current) by touching the metal with an electrode (an electrode is a type of tool, usually made of metal, that conducts electric current). The welder guides the electrode along the metal seams until the heat of the arc melts the metal.

Gas welding is the most commonly used process; its flexibility makes it popular in almost all kinds of metalworking. The flame that the welder uses comes from a mixture of oxygen and a combustible gas. To get the right flame size and quality, the welder must adjust the oxygen and gas valves on the torch, then hold the flame against the metal until it melts. The welding rod is then applied to the molten metal to form the weld that holds the pieces together.

Finally, resistance welding gets its heat source from resistance by the work piece to an electric current and from pressure. Resistance welding is a machine process used in the mass production of various kinds of manufacturing parts.

Many welders plan their work by reviewing drawings or blueprints, then use various types of welding equipment to either produce new metal pieces or to repair damaged ones. Some workers use automatic welding machines, setting them up and operating them according to specifications for each job.

Working conditions for welders are often considered potentially hazardous. They must wear protective clothing, safety shoes, goggles, hard hats, and sometimes other gear to protect themselves from falling objects and to avoid burns and eye injuries. Also, because some metals give off toxic gas and fumes as they are melted, the working area must always be properly ventilated.

Education and training

For all welding jobs, employers look for workers who have good manual dexterity and good eyesight. For skilled jobs (including maintenance work, where welders travel to construction sites or utility plants to do repairs) a high school or vocational school diploma is preferred. Classwork should include mathematics, mechanical drawing, physics, and shopwork.

To become a welder, a person must usually complete an on-the-job training program. The length of training time varies from several weeks for most resistance welding jobs to between one and three years for skilled arc and gas welding jobs.

Earnings

In general, job opportunities for welders are not expected to be very good during the 1990s. Many tasks are done by robots these days, and this is expected to continue. The best opportunities will probably be for maintenance and repair work.

Average hourly earnings of welders depend on the skill required, as well as on the industry or activity in which the welder is employed. The average annual pay for welders in the 1990s ranged from about $20,800 to $26,000. Some workers earned more than $32,000 per year.

Ways of getting more information

To enter the welding trade, applicants should contact a manufacturing plant, the state employment service bureau, or the local branch of the appropriate union.

For more information about the work of welders write to the following agencies:

▶ Wearing a protective mask, a welder joins two pieces of metal with a small blowtorch.

▶ American Welding Society
PO Box 351040
550 LeJeune Road, NW
Miami, FL 33135

▶ International Association of Machinists and Aerospace Workers
1300 Connecticut Avenue
Washington, DC 20036

Wholesale Sales Workers

Other articles to look at:
- ▶ **Buyers**
- ▶ **Manufacturers' Sales Representatives**
- ▶ **Retail Sales Workers**
- ▶ **Retail Store Managers**

What wholesale sales workers do

Wholesale sales workers sell products to buyers in retail stores and in commercial or industrial companies. These sales workers do not work for the manufacturer of the products. Instead, they work for wholesaling companies that buy from the manufacturer and sell to the retailer.

Wholesale sales workers may sell a great variety of products. Some sell air conditioners, refrigerators, or freezers. Others may sell all the medicines that a drug company produces. All sales workers, however, try to give their customers as much service and support as possible. For instance, they may help the retail buyer to set up a store display, to plan advertising, and to find out about buying trends. The sales worker may also write up orders, make sure the products are delivered, arrange for payment, prepare reports of sales and expenses, and solve any problems the buyer may have.

Most wholesale sales workers specialize in a certain type of product. Also, many work in one region or district. By visiting the same customers regularly, they get to know their customers' needs. Much of a wholesale sales worker's time is spent traveling from one customer to another. Some products sell more at one time of year than at another, so sales workers sometimes suffer periods of low work activity.

Education and training

Wholesale employers prefer to hire applicants who have at least a high school education. A degree from a junior college can help an applicant get a better job in the wholesale field. Some high school courses that are useful for future wholesale sales workers are English, bookkeeping, economics, typing, office procedures, and sales-related courses. These courses can be taken in college, too, along with marketing, wholesaling, retailing, advertising, and accounting. A college degree is often required for jobs in specialized fields or for advancement to higher positions. Wholesalers who work with medicines and drugs, for instance, might need to have a biology or pharmacy degree.

No special licenses are required to work as a wholesale sales worker. Having experience in the wholesale field or in other sales areas is the best way to get a job and to advance. High school graduates may apply directly to wholesale employers listed in the telephone directory. College graduates or experienced workers in other fields may learn of openings through employment services, guidance counselors, or sales associations.

▶ Placing an order over the phone, a wholesale sales worker obtains items to be sold in large quantities to stores.

Earnings

Throughout the 1990s job openings will arise as the economy grows and as new products come onto the market.

When wholesale sales workers begin a job, they usually receive either a salary or a combination of salary and commission (a percentage of the price of an item sold). In the 1990s, wholesale sales workers earned an average of $28,000 a year. Most earned between $19,900 and $41,400 per year, while some made as much as $51,000.

Ways of getting more information

For more information write to:

▶ Nat'l. Assoc. of Wholesaler-Distributors
  1725 K Street, NW
  Washington, DC 20006

▶ Sales and Marketing Executives Int'l.
  Statler Office Tower, No. 458
  Cleveland, OH 44115

Winemakers

Other articles to look at:
► **Agricultural Scientists**
► **Dietetic Technicians**
► **Farmers**
► **Food Technologists**

What winemakers do

Enology—better known as winemaking—is more than five thousand years old, certainly one of the world's oldest professions. The ancient Egyptians, Greeks, Romans, and Chinese all used wine for either medicinal or religious purposes or just to drink with a meal. Grapes for winemaking have been grown in the United States since the late 1800s, and winemaking here is now a major industry, especially in California, where more than 80 percent of U.S. wines are produced.

Winemakers are involved in all phases of wine production and must have a thorough understanding of the business. As an expert in viticulture (the growing of grapes), the enologist has many important decisions to make. Perhaps the most important decision is which grapes to grow. There are thousands of varieties of grapes, and they differ in such aspects as color, size, and shape. Winemakers study the different European and American grapes and then decide which varieties are best for the soil and climate of their land. For example, a winemaker in the Napa Valley of California would need to make sure the grapes planted could withstand very hot summers, while in upstate New York grapes need to survive extremely cold winters. The variety of grape that is grown determines when to plant, when to prune, and when to pick.

The winemaker must keep up-to-date on new technology that comes along to help the winemaking process. For example, he or she might have to decide on whether to use highly mechanical grape harvesters and crushers, which speed up the entire winemaking process but might distort the quality. The winemaker also has to consult with staff members about the testing and crushing of the grapes and their cooling, filtering, and bottling.

As the winery's business manager, the winemaker must have certain expertise in financial matters; for example, he or she must have the ability to analyze profit-and-loss statements and other parts of balance sheets. Winemakers are also involved with the marketing of the wines, including making such crucial decisions as where the wines will be sold and at what price. They usually oversee all matters involving their staffs—for example, hiring and firing and setting salaries. Winemakers are top-level managers who have final responsibility for the success of their wineries.

Education and training

Winemaking is an increasingly competitive field, and a college degree is often needed to obtain an entry-level job. High school course work should emphasize biology, chemistry, and other sciences, and the college major should be in either viticulture or horticulture. In addition, business and computer courses should be a part of the student's college program.

Advancement within the profession depends on a combination of education, experience, and skill. Winemakers at small wineries may move on to become managers of large ones, and they in turn may become directors of several wineries that are part of a large corporation. Because of the small number of wineries, however, and because enologists are already high-level managers, opportunities for advancement are limited.

Earnings

Wine has become very popular in the United States since the 1960s and 1970s, and this trend is expected to continue. There should be many job opportunities for prospective winemakers. Most jobs are and will continue to be in California, specifically in the San Joaquin, Napa, and Sonoma valleys. There are many opportunities for part-time and summer jobs at most good-sized wineries. Working at a winery even for a short time will help a prospective winemaker decide if he or she has the skill and outlook needed for this career.

Beginning salary levels depend on the applicant's education level and the size of the winery. The average beginning salary is between $18,000 and $28,000 per year. Experienced winemakers earn between $30,000 and $85,000 per year.

▶ Testing during the aging process is one of the skills needed by winemakers to make sure the wine is aging well.

For more information on a career in making wine, write to the following agencies:

▶ American Society for Enology and Viticulture
  PO Box 1855
  Davis, CA 95617

▶ American Wine Society
  3006 Latta Road
  Rochester, NY 14612

Ways of getting more information

Many wineries give tours, and taking a tour is a useful way to observe the profession close up.

Wood Science and Technology Careers

Other articles to look at:
▶ **Agricultural Engineers**
▶ **Construction Workers**
▶ **Foresters**
▶ **Forestry Technicians**
▶ **Papermaking Occupations**

What wood scientists and technologists do

There are three major career areas in the wood science and technology field. These are *wood scientist, wood technologist,* and *wood products technician.* All three study and test wood and products made out of wood.

Wood scientists try to find new ways to dry, preserve, and make things out of wood. They may develop new ways to dry wood, or cure it, so that it will last longer. For example, one way to dry wood planks is to heat them in large ovens called kilns. Some wood scientists study and improve this heating process. They try to find ways to keep the wood from splitting or bending as it is drying. Other wood scientists develop chemicals that will protect the wood from insects or fire or from rotting. Still others test different kinds of wood to see how they can best be used.

Wood technologists, also called *wood products engineers,* often work for lumber or paper industries. They test wood-related materials and equipment, such as kilns, sawmill machin-ery, and pulp machines. They may also test woods for strength and develop new ways to glue wood. Some wood technologists give advice to home builders about what kinds of wood to use for doors, floors, or outdoor decks.

Wood products technicians work for companies that make wood products. They oversee the operation of kilns, saws, wood presses, and other equipment and make sure they are in good working order. Wood products technicians are problem solvers, too. They may run tests on wood to make sure of its quality. Often they give their employers advice on how to process wood more efficiently.

Working conditions for wood science workers vary. Many do research work in laboratories. Travel is often required for those who buy or sell wood for their employers. Many wood technologists and technicians work in sawmills or processing plants, where the work may be noisy or dirty.

Education and training

Wood scientists and technologists should have a bachelor's degree with a major in forest products or wood technology. Other acceptable degrees are chemistry, engineering, physics, biology, and civil or mechanical engineering. With these degrees, however, it is still important to take courses in wood science. Some wood science courses include wood anatomy, wood structure, wood physics, and wood chemistry. Wood products technicians must have at least a certificate or an associate degree from a two-year college. High school students interested in a career in wood science or technology should take mathematics, English, and science courses such as physics, chemistry, and biology.

Earnings

Between 1985 and the year 2000, the need for wood products is expected to have doubled. Thus, there will be a tremendous demand for wood scientists, technologists, and technicians throughout the 1990s.

In the 1990s, wood scientists and technologists with a bachelor's degree earned a beginning salary of about $16,500 to $22,000 a year. Those working for the federal government began at $17,824 and after a long career earned as much as $52,262 a year. Wood scientists and technologists with a doctorate started at $27,500 to $33,000 per year. The average yearly salary for experienced wood products technicians in the 1990s was about $22,000. Starting salary for these technicians ranged from $13,200 to $17,600 per year.

Ways of getting more information

Young people interested in wood science and technology careers may be able to take a tour or a field trip to a sawmill, paper plant, or wood processing plant in their area. They may also learn about wood and how to work with it through a wood shop or woodworking course in high school or a local vocational school or community college.

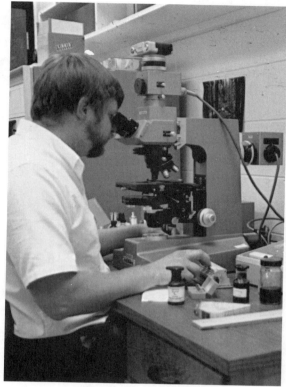

▶ A wood scientist stains wood samples to check for damage done to the fibers during processing.

For more information about wood science, wood technology, or forestry careers, write to:

▶ Society of American Foresters
5400 Grosvenor Lane
Bethesda, MD 20814

▶ Society of Wood Science and Technology
One Gifford Pinchot Drive
Madison, WI 53705

Word Processor Operators

Other articles to look at:
- ► **Computer Programmers**
- ► **Computer-Service Technicians**
- ► **Office-Machine Servicers**
- ► **Systems Analysts**
- ► **Typists**

What word processor operators do

Word processor operators use computers to type handwritten or tape-recorded material and put it in final form. Word processor operators can produce letters, legal documents, reports, or charts on their machines. The keyboard on which they type is similar to the keyboard of a typewriter. Whatever the operator types appears lit up on a screen, much like a small TV screen, called a video display terminal, or a VDT. As the operator types, the word processor's computer stores the material on a tape or a disk. The operator can correct any mistakes, add material, or make changes instantly to a document before making a final copy.

As the operators type in material, they also type in directions for the computer. For example, some symbols may tell the computer to underline a certain sentence or to put the title in the center of the paper. The operator can have the word processor line up numbers in columns to make a chart, put the material in letter form, or create bar or line graphs.

When the document is typed in, corrected, and arranged in the proper form, the word processor electronically transfers the document to a printer that prints it out. The operator only has to type a document once; the printer can then make as many copies as the operator needs. If the operator needs to send a form letter to hundreds of people, she can direct the word processor to type hundreds of copies of the letter, changing only the address on each one.

All kinds of offices—law firms, government agencies, hospitals, stores, and other businesses—employ word processing operators. These employees usually work in comfortable and well-lighted offices, sitting at desks or tables most of the day.

Many operators work 35 to 40 hours a week, although they may have to work overtime on rush projects. Some offices have two work shifts, one during the day and one in the evening, so that operators can be working on the word processors as much as possible.

Education and training

Word processor operators must finish high school. High school courses in typing and using office machines are absolutely necessary. They also must understand grammar rules and be good spellers.

Some employers will train new employees on word processors. It takes from three to six months to become skilled at operating a word processor; operators need to type 45 to 80 words a minute. Most employers prefer to hire those who have already learned how to use word processors.

▶ Entering information into a computer, a word processor operator prepares a document for storing and reprinting.

Earnings

Throughout the 1990s, job opportunities for word processor operators are not expected to increase very much. Although the amount of text that needs to be processed is increasing, advances in new automatic equipment allow the work to be done faster, with fewer workers.

The average yearly salary for word processor operators is about $18,000. Salaries tend to vary among different industries; they are generally higher in transportation and utilities companies and lower in finance, insurance, and real estate firms.

Ways of getting more information

For more information write to:

▶ Data Processing Management Association
505 Busse Highway
Park Ridge, IL 60068

▶ Professional Secretaries International
10502 NW Ambassador Drive
Kansas City, MO 64195

Writers and Authors

Other articles to look at:
► **Book Editors**
► **Magazine Editors**
► **Reporters and Correspondents**
► **Technical Writers**

What writers and authors do

Writers and *authors* express their ideas in written form for such media as books, magazines, newspapers, advertisements, and radio and television. Writers' and authors' jobs are a combination of creativity and hard work.

Because the field of writing is so broad, workers usually specialize in a particular type of writing. For example, those who prepare scripts for motion pictures or television are called *screenwriters* or *scriptwriters*. *Playwrights* do similar writing but for theater. Those who write copy for advertisements are called *copywriters*.

Newswriters prepare stories for newspapers, radio, and TV. *Columnists* specialize in writing about matters from their personal viewpoints. *Critics* review and comment upon the work of other authors, musicians, artists, and performers.

In addition to all of these types of writers, there are also *technical writers, novelists, biographers, poets, essayists, comedy writers,* and *short story writers.*

Many authors write about matters that have captured their imagination. Although sometimes a publisher or editor will ask an author to write something to suit the needs of a particular publication, authors often write things because they want to be creative. Authors are somewhat different in this regard from journalists, copywriters, and others who are normally assigned topics.

Good writers gather as much information as possible about a subject and then carefully check the accuracy of their sources. Usually, this involves extensive library research and interviews or long hours of observation and personal experience. Writers keep notes from which they prepare an outline. They often rewrite sections of the material, always searching for the best way to express an idea or opinion. A manuscript may be reviewed, corrected, and revised many times before a final copy is ready.

Education and training

A college education is necessary if you want to become a writer, as is an ability to type and handle the pressure of deadlines. Some employers prefer to hire people who have a communications or journalism degree. Others require majors in English, literature, history, philosophy, or one of the social sciences. Technical writers should have a background in engineering, business, computers, or one of the sciences.

Many authors have learned their skill on their own, practicing the creative art of writing. Joining a writing group or class is a helpful way to learn how to sharpen skills and understand the writing process. Classes and groups can be found almost anywhere, from community colleges to park districts.

Earnings

Salaried employment opportunities in writing are expected to be very good during the 1990s. Jobs should be available at newspapers, periodicals, book publishers, and non-profit organizations, Opportunities are expected to be especially good for technical writers. However, competition for jobs is very intense.

The job market for authors of books is difficult to predict. Because they are usually self-employed, much of their success depends on the amount and type of work created and their ability to sell that work. There really is no average salary for an author. Most set their own hours and prices. Some authors get grants to allow them to do their writing; others win prizes and awards.

Beginning writers' salaries range from $18,000 to $26,600 per year. More experienced writers may earn between $20,800 and $37,900. A few best-selling authors may make $100,000 or more per year.

Ways of getting more information

A good way to find out about being an author is to write a story or some poetry in school or at home. Enter it in a writing contest or submit it to a local newspaper or school yearbook. Also, visit a publishing company, newspaper, or magazine office and ask the staff writers about their work.

For more information write to:

▶ Dow Jones Newspaper Fund
   PO Box 300
   Princeton, NJ 08543

▶ Women in Communications
   2101 Wilson Boulevard, Suite 417
   Arlington, VA 22201

▶ Well-known writers, such as Toni Morrison, often attend book signings to promote their latest work.

161

X-Ray Technologists

Other articles to look at:
▶ **Biomedical Engineers**
▶ **Electromechanical Technicians**
▶ **Medical Technologists**
▶ **Nuclear Instrumentation Technicians**
▶ **Physicians**

What X-ray technologists do

X-ray technologists work under the supervision of a physician known as a *radiologist* to help diagnose and treat diseases using X rays and radioactive material.

In regular photography, images are made by exposing a specially treated photographic plate to ordinary light rays. In radiography, or X-ray photography, images are made by exposing the plates to special short light rays, called X rays. Because all forms of radiation are potentially harmful, great care must be taken when using X rays. Some X-ray technologists specialize in diagnostic medicine—in figuring out exactly what disease a patient has, and which part of the body it is affecting. These technologists operate the X-ray machines that produce images of bones, tissues, and organs inside the body. When evaluated by the radiologist, the images can be used to locate broken bones, identify diseased tissues, or pinpoint cancerous tumors and other growths.

Other X-ray technologists specialize in therapeutic work. Radiation therapy uses the effect of radiation to destroy diseased body tissue, and carefully controlled and precisely directed doses of radiation are used to treat some tumors. Working under the direction of radiologists and other physicians, these technologists expose patients to X rays directed at the diseased body parts.

Some X-ray technologists practice both diagnostic and therapeutic radiology. Others may specialize in such areas as nuclear medicine, where radioactive compounds are injected into or swallowed by the patient to diagnose and treat certain conditions, or sonography, where sound waves instead of light waves are used to project an image.

Whatever their specialty, X-ray technologists must be skilled in using potentially dangerous instruments and substances, and must always keep the patient's comfort and safety in mind. And whether employed by hospitals, physicians' and dentists' offices, clinics, laboratories, or government agencies, these workers should be both physically and emotionally healthy themselves, and should have a desire to work with the injured and ill.

Education and training

Prospective X-ray technologists need a high school education and must then go on to complete a formal education program in radiographic technology. There are hundreds of such programs in the United States, offered by hospitals, medical schools, colleges, and universities. These programs last anywhere from two to four years. Some programs re-

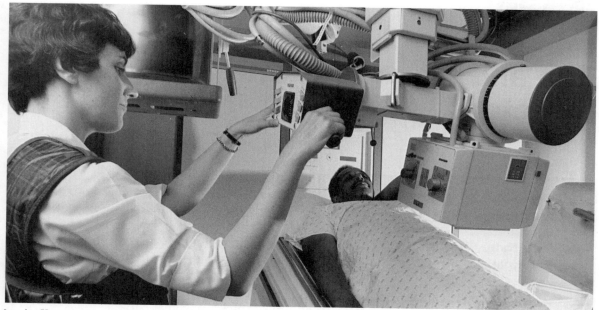

▶ An X-ray technologist positions the machine over the patient.

quire one or two years of higher education beyond high school. An increasing number of states have licensing requirements for X-ray technologists, and it is anticipated that in the future all workers will need to be accredited.

Earnings

The future looks excellent for these skilled technologists, as radiology is being used more and more in diagnosing and treating disease.

The starting salary for X-ray technologists in a hospital, medical school, or medical center averaged about $18,500 annually in the 1990s, while experienced technologists earned an average of $27,800 per year.

Ways of getting more information

For more information write to the following organizations:

▶ American Registry of Radiologic Technologists
1255 Northland Drive
Mendota Heights, MN 55120

▶ Society of Diagnostic Medical Sonographers
12225 Greenville Avenue
Dallas, TX 75243

Zoo and Aquarium Curators and Directors

Other articles to look at:
- ▶ **Biologists**
- ▶ **Ecologists**
- ▶ **Park Naturalists**
- ▶ **Veterinarians**
- ▶ **Zoologists**

What zoo and aquarium curators and directors do

Zoo curators and *aquarium curators* are the people in charge of the care and survival of the animals at the zoo or aquarium where they work. Curators need to have expert knowledge of the housing requirements, daily care, medical plans, dietary needs, and social habits of the animals in their care. They work closely with keepers, veterinarians, exhibit designers, educators, and with the director of their facility. They supervise the daily activities of the keepers and oversee important behavioral research that determines whether the animals are getting enough activity and whether they are thriving in their social groupings. They are also involved in dietary research to make sure the animals are eating the best foods for their health.

Another very important mission of curators is to make sure that endangered species can survive in captivity, with the hope that the species will grow in number and eventually be able to live in the wild again. Curators devise species survival plans, which include sched- ules for where specific animals will live, who their mates should be, and where their offspring should be raised.

Large zoos and aquariums often have a general curator to oversee the entire collection of animals, plus a curator for each division. For instance, a large zoo might have a general curator, a bird curator, a reptile curator, and a mammal curator.

Zoo directors and *aquarium directors* are the heads of zoos and aquariums. They need to have some knowledge of animals, but they are more involved in the business management of their institution. A director is like the mayor of a city. He or she is in charge of fund-raising, administrative matters, and public relations, but isn't necessarily involved in the day-to-day care of the animals. While curators typically have a background in science, directors are more likely to have a background in accounting, business, or fund-raising.

Education and training

A curator needs to have at least a bachelor's degree in one of the biological sciences, such as zoology or biology, but a master's degree is often required and a doctorate is needed to work in large institutions. A lengthy background in hands-on experience is also vital for people wanting to become curators. Many people who are curators today started out by volunteering as a zookeeper and working their way up over the years while simultaneously getting their education.

▶ Working closely with the zookeeper, the curator oversees important behavioral, dietary, and medical research with zoo animals.

People who are interested in becoming zoo or aquarium directors need a well-rounded education with at least a bachelor's degree.

Earnings

Jobs as curators and directors are tough to find and very competitive. Those who have the best credentials and who demonstrate a keen knowledge of animals and a willingness to work hard are most likely to succeed.

The average salary of a curator is hard to determine with salaries ranging from $20,000 to $75,000.

Zoo and aquarium directors are also paid a wide range of salaries, but as the highest paid officials in their institutions, they generally earn anywhere from $25,000 to $75,000; a few directors in large metropolitan areas earn $100,000 or more.

Ways of getting more information

Volunteering is one of the best ways to find out whether the work is enjoyable.

For further information, write to:

▶ American Association of Zoological Parks and Aquariums Conservation Center
7970D Old Georgetown Road
Bethesda, MD 20814

165

Zookeepers

Other articles to look at:
- ▶ **Animal Health Technicians**
- ▶ **Dairy Farmers**
- ▶ **Equestrian Management**
- ▶ **Veterinary Technicians**
- ▶ **Zoo and Aquarium Curators and Directors**

What zookeepers do

Zookeepers are the workers who take care of animals at a zoo day and night. Their responsibilities include preparing the animals' food and giving it to them, cleaning their cages, moving animals from one location to another, and making improvements in their living conditions as needed. Such improvements might include putting in new bars and ropes for monkeys to swing on.

Another very important duty of zookeepers is to watch the animals they're in charge of very closely for any signs of sickness or injury, such as changes in eating habits, sleeping patterns, or behavior. They also keep close track of any mating habits. Each day, zookeepers write down what they've observed about the animals in a logbook. In addition, they may feed and help raise baby animals as well as take care of sick animals. Zookeepers may also help design and build the enclosures for animals and take care of the surrounding environment, such as plants and trees.

Some zookeepers have rotating schedules: one week they may care for monkeys and an-telopes and the next they'll care for lions and giraffes. This kind of rotation makes a keeper's job more interesting and educational and it's also good for the animals, so that they'll be accustomed to a number of different people. Other zookeepers become specialists and work with just one group of animals, such as elephants or exotic birds.

Zookeepers not only need to be knowledgeable about the animals they're caring for, but also very responsible people who are committed to the animals day in and day out and who will always treat them well and with great patience. They have to be willing to do hard and sometimes dirty physical work, often in bad weather conditions. Sometimes they are at risk of being injured, and it is very important to follow safety procedures very carefully, to stay alert, and to remain calm in the event of an emergency.

Since animals need 24-hour care, keepers have to be willing to work odd hours, including nights, weekends, and holidays. Keepers also need to be friendly and have good communications skills, because they often talk to the public and answer questions about the animals.

Education and training

The minimum requirement for a job as a zookeeper is a high school diploma. Completion of a one or two-year training program in animal care in a vocational school or junior college is also recommended. More and more zookeepers today have a bachelor's degree in a science such as zoology.

People interested in becoming zookeepers need to have experience working with animals. They can get this experience by volunteering at a zoo, working on a farm, or helping care for animals at a vet's or a kennel.

Earnings

While there are more keepers than any other kind of employee at a zoo or wildlife park or aquarium, these positions are nevertheless few in number, and openings are hard to find. Only about 350 keeper jobs become available each year in the United States, and there are usually many candidates for each job.

However, as the preservation of animal species becomes more complicated and more challenging, zoos, aquariums, and wildlife parks will become increasingly important. For this reason, the future for careers in zoo work is fairly promising, especially for those who are truly dedicated.

Depending on their geographical location and level of experience, zookeepers may earn as little as $10,000 per year to as much as $20,000. Those who advance to senior or lead keepers will make the most.

Ways of getting more information

A good way to learn about what it's like to work at a zoo is to visit zoos, aquariums or parks where animals are raised. The keepers and other workers should be happy to answer questions.

All zoos need volunteers, and many offer volunteer programs for students who can work part-time or during the summer. Another way to get direct experience with animals is to take care of animals on a farm or join a 4-H club.

▶ Tending to an elephant's mouth, this zookeeper looks closely for any signs of sickness.

For further information write to:

▶ American Association of Zoo Keepers
  Topeka Zoological Park
  635 Gage Boulevard
  Topeka, KS 66606

▶ Humane Society of the United States
  2100 L Street, N.W.
  Washington, DC 20037

167

Zoologists

Other articles to look at:
▶ **Biologists**
▶ **Ecologists**
▶ **Naturalists**
▶ **Park Naturalists**
▶ **Zoo and Aquarium Curators and Directors**

What zoologists do

Zoology is another word for animal biology. *Zoologists* study all areas of animal life, including the origins of animals, their behavior, diseases, and life processes.

Zoologists are further named by the animal group they study: *ornithologists* study birds, *mammalogists* study mammals, *herpetologists* study reptiles, and *ichthyologists* study fish. There are many other types of zoologists, including *entomologists, marine biologists,* and *physiologists*.

The specific jobs of zoologists depend not only on their animal speciality, but on whether they're involved in basic research, applied research, teaching, administration, or another field. Zoologists have a great deal of curiousity about nature and science and possess good observational abilities.

Those working in basic research may conduct experiments on live or dead animals, in a laboratory or in natural surroundings, in order to make discoveries that might help humans. Such research in the past has led to advances in nutrition and to an increased understanding in such fields as aging, reproduction, food production, and pest control. This type of research can also be controversial, or unpopular, because it sometimes involves killing animals or treating them in ways that some people find cruel and inhumane. Because of this, researchers must uphold very strict lab standards.

Zoologists in applied research may use the findings of basic researchers and apply them to solve specific problems in such fields as medicine, conservation, and aquarium and zoo work. For example, applied researchers may develop a new drug for people or animals, a new pesticide, or a new type of pet food. Some research zoologists work in the field with wild animals such as whales, tracing their movements with radio transmitters and observing their behavior, eating habits, mating patterns, and so on. Researchers use all kinds of laboratory chemicals and equipment such as dissecting tools, microscopes, slides, electron microscopes, and other sophisticated machinery.

Other zoologists teach in colleges and universities while conducting their own research for publication. Like most university faculty members, they may teach classes from nine to 16 hours a week and spend the rest of their work time supervising the laboratory work of students or helping them with field projects. Other zoologists hold administrative or managerial jobs in zoos and aquariums. Still others work for government agencies, private businesses, and independent research organizations. A few are self-employed.

▶ Gently helping a giant tortoise swim, the zoologist is careful not to touch the healing neck sore.

Education and training

Students interested in becoming zoologists should take high school courses in the biological and physical sciences. Zoologists not only need a bachelor's degree, but a master's or doctoral degree is almost always required for jobs involving research or teaching. Typical college coursework includes classes in organic and inorganic chemistry, physics, mathematics, statistics, computer science, and English, as well as extensive lab work and training in laboratory techniques.

Earnings

Employment opportunities for zoologists are expected to be better in private industry than in the federal government in the 1990s.

Starting salaries for zoologists with a bachelor's degree range from $16,000 to $20,000 per year. Those with a master's degree earn starting salaries ranging from $20,000 to $24,000, and those with a doctorate can earn a starting salary of $28,000 to $35,000. Experienced zoologists can earn $50,000 or more.

Ways of getting more information

For further information, write to:

▶ American Society of Zoologists
104 Sirius Circle
Thousand Oaks, CA 91360

Index to Skills Groupings

Manual Skills

People Skills

Science and Mathematical Skills

Social Science Skills

Glossary

accredited Approved as meeting established standards for providing good training and education. This approval is usually given by an independent organization of professionals to a school or a program in a school. Compare **certified** and **licensed.**

apprentice A person who is learning a trade by working under the supervision of a skilled worker. Apprentices often receive classroom instruction in addition to their supervised practical experience.

apprenticeship **1.** A program for training apprentices (see **apprentice**). **2.** The period of time when a person is an apprentice. In highly skilled trades, apprenticeships may last three or four years.

associate degree An academic rank or title granted by a community or junior college or similar institution to graduates of a two-year program of education beyond high school.

bachelor's degree An academic rank or title given to a person who has completed a four-year program of study at a college or university. Also called an *undergraduate degree.*

certified Approved as meeting established requirements for skill, knowledge, and experience in a particular field. People are certified by the organization of professionals in their field. Compare **accredited** and **licensed.**

commission A percentage of the money taken in by a company in sales that is given to the salesperson as pay, either in addition to or instead of a salary.

community college A public two-year college, attended by students who do not live at the college. Graduates of a community college receive an associate degree and may transfer to a four-year college or university to complete a bachelor's degree. Compare **junior college** and **technical community college.**

curriculum All the courses available in a school or college; or, the courses offered in a particular subject.

degree An academic title given by a college or university to a student who has completed a program of study.

diploma A certificate or document given by a school to show that a person has completed a course or has graduated from the school.

doctorate An academic rank or title (the highest) granted by a graduate school to a person who has completed a two- to three-year program after having received a master's degree.

engineering The profession that is concerned with ways of making practical use of scientific knowledge. Typical engineering activities include planning and managing the building of bridges, dams, roads, chemical plants, machinery, and new industrial products.

freelancer A self-employed person who contracts to do specific jobs.

fringe benefit A payment or benefit to an employee in addition to regular wages or salary. Examples of fringe benefits include a pension, a paid vacation, and health or life insurance.

graduate school A school that people may attend after they have received their bachelor's degree. People who successfully complete an educational program at a graduate school earn a master's degree or a doctorate.

humanities The branches of learning that are concerned with language, the arts, literature, philosophy, and history.

intern An advanced student (usually one with at least some college training) in a professional field who is employed in a job that is intended to provide supervised practical experience to the student.

internship **1.** The position or job of an intern (see **intern**). **2.** The period of time when a person is an intern.

journeyman A person who has completed an apprenticeship or other training period and is qualified to work in a trade.

junior college A two-year college that offers courses like those in the first half of a four-year college program. Graduates of a junior college usually receive an associate degree and may transfer to a four-year college or university to complete a bachelor's degree. Compare **community college.**

labor **1.** Employees of a company other than those in management. **2.** The organizations (such as unions) representing groups of employees.

liberal arts The liberal arts include philosophy, literature, music, fine arts, history, language, and social sciences.

licensed Having formal permission from the proper authority to carry out an activity that would be illegal without that permission. For example, a person may be licensed to practice medicine or to drive a car. Compare **certified.**

life sciences The natural sciences that are concerned with living organisms and the processes that take place within them (see **natural sciences).**

major (in college) The academic field in which a student specializes and receives a degree.

master's degree An academic rank or title granted by a graduate school to a person who has completed a one- or two-year program after having received a bachelor's degree.

natural sciences All the sciences that are concerned with the objects and processes in nature that can be measured. The natural sciences include biology, chemistry, and geology.

pension An amount of money paid regularly by an employer to a former employee after he or she retires from working.

personnel 1. The group of people who are employed in a company or institution. **2.** The department within an organization that is concerned with employees, especially hiring them.

physical sciences The natural sciences that are concerned mainly with nonliving matter, including physics, chemistry, and astronomy.

private 1. Not owned or controlled by the government (such as private industry or a private employment agency). **2.** Intended only for a particular person or group; not open to all (such as a private road or a private club).

public 1. Provided or operated by the government (such as a public library). **2.** Open and available to everyone (such as public meeting).

regulatory Having to do with the rules and laws for carrying out an activity. A regulatory agency, for example, is a government organization that sets up required procedures for how certain things should be done.

scholarship A gift of money to a student to help the student pay for further education.

social sciences The branches of learning (such as economics and political science) that are concerned with the behavior of groups of human beings.

social studies Courses of study (such as civics, geography, and history) that deal with how human societies work.

starting salary The salary paid to a newly hired employee. The starting salary is usually a smaller amount than is paid to a more experienced worker.

technical college A private or public college offering two- or four-year programs in technical subjects. Technical colleges offer courses in both general and technical subjects and award associate degrees and bachelor's degrees. Compare **technical community college.**

technical community college A community college that provides training for technicians (see **community college).** Technical community colleges offer courses in both general and technical subjects and award associate degrees. Compare **technical college.**

technical institute A public or private school that offers training in technical subjects. Technical institutes usually offer only a few courses in general subjects and do not award any kind of degree. Technical institutes that offer a broader range of subjects and award degrees are usually called **technical colleges** or **technical community colleges.**

technical school A general term used to describe technical colleges, technical community colleges, and technical institutes. Compare **trade school** and **vocational school.**

trade An occupation that requires training and skills in working with one's hands.

trade school A public or private school that offers training in one or more of the trades (see **trade).** Compare **technical school** and **vocational school.**

undergraduate A student at a college or university who has not yet received a degree.

undergraduate degree See **bachelor's degree.**

union An organization whose members are workers in a particular industry or company. The union works to gain better wages, benefits, and working conditions for its members. Also called a *labor union* or *trade union.*

vocational school A public or private school that offers training in one or more skills or trades. Compare **technical school** and **trade school.**

wage Money that is paid in return for work done, especially money paid on the basis of the number of hours or days worked.

Photo Credits

Index

189

DATE DUE

JUL 2 1 1997			
APR 1 3 1998			
NOV 5 2001			

DEMCO 38-297